Best Practices Series

How to Sell New Business and Expand Existing Business

The Practitioner's Guide to Rainmaking for Professional Service Firms

Alan Weiss, Ph.D.

KENNEDY INFORMATION

FITZWILLIAM, NEW HAMPSHIRE

ISBN 1-885922-88-4

Special thanks to David Hamacher and Kathleen Hassan for their contribution to the CD that accompanies this book.

The Consultants News Best Practices Series by Alan Weiss, Ph.D

Book 1: How to Write a Proposal That's Accepted Every Time

Book 2: How to Market, Establish a Brand, and Sell Professional Services

Book 3: How to Sell New Business and Expand Existing Business

These books may be ordered from Kennedy Information, One Kennedy Place, Fitzwilliam, NH 03447.

1-800-531-0007 or 603-585-3101   E-mail: *bookstore@kennedyinfo.com*

www.consultingcentral.com

About the Author

Alan Weiss is an internationally recognized consultant, speaker, and author. He is the president of Summit Consulting Group Inc., a firm he founded in 1985. His clients have included Merck, Mercedes-Benz, Hewlett-Packard, The Federal Reserve Bank, and more than 200 other major organizations around the world. He is the author of 17 books, including his best-selling *Million Dollar Consulting,* considered the seminal work on growing a consulting practice.

The *New York Post* has called Dr. Weiss "one of the most highly respected independent consultants in the country," and *Success* magazine has cited him as "a worldwide expert in executive education" in an editorial devoted to his work. You can write to him at Alan@summitconsulting.com, and you will find more than 60 indexed, complementary articles and other resources on his Web site: http://www.summitconsulting.com.

The author wishes to acknowledge the generous help and support provided in this and other ventures by the wonderful people at Kennedy Information.

Contents

Part Two: Expanding Business

Why We Created a Book about Acquiring Business

Most professionals who provide services—consultants, Realtors, architects, trainers, facilitators, executive search experts, attorneys, and others—don't realize that they're actually in the marketing business. I've seen superb professionals with terrific methodologies fail at their calling because they are terrible at "making rain." I've seen average professionals succeed quite nicely with mediocre approaches because they were adept at making rain.

And I've seen superb professionals who are terrific at making rain also make a fortune.

Whether you are a solo practitioner, a small firm principal, or an employee of a large firm, our intent here is to provide a pragmatic and specific guide to both acquiring new business and securing repeat business. One of the cardinal sins of the sales profession is to "leave money on the table." A second, equally grave, is to fail to gain the "annuities" that repeat business provides.

Since we are all investing in the cost of acquisition—and some of us investing to the point that anything short of a huge sale is nonprofitable—we had better become adept at identifying the value proposition, the buyer, and the "hot buttons." And we had also better get good at speeding the velocity of the sale. From initial lead to final signed proposal, that timing must be consistently compressed.

As has been our custom in our earlier books in this series (*How to Write a Proposal That's Accepted Every Time* and *How to Market, Establish a Brand, and Sell Professional Services*), we have chosen a large format for ease of reading, reference, and notes. A conventional format would have resulted in a 200-page paperback (400 pages, if we had included the notes sections). We've learned, however, that readers prefer to highlight, write in the margins, make notes across from key issues, and generally use the book as a reference manual.

I've held back nothing. Everything I know about proposal writing, branding, marketing, and selling is in this series. While there are many fine sources available, a reader could create an entire business marketing plan and implementation steps just from this concise library. And that is exactly what my friends at Kennedy Information and I intend.

I can't guarantee that these techniques will increase your sales, because I can't control your talent or your discipline. I can tell you, however, that the techniques have worked for me in a variety of *Fortune* 100 and international organizations, public and private, profit and nonprofit.

Improve by 1 percent a day, and in 70 days you'll be twice as good. I call that my Tools for Change: The 1% Solution™. I'm betting you'll find at least that 1 percent within these pages, and maybe every single day.

—Alan Weiss, Ph.D., CMC
East Greenwich, RI
November 2001

Part I

Acquiring New Business

Chapter 1

The Art of the Sale: What Is Selling?

Does this mean I have to deal with people?

Selling is the gaining of agreement from the buyer to accept a product or service that fills a legitimate, perceived need in return for agreed-upon compensation in a certain form on a certain date for the seller.

Any questions?

"Selling" became important commercially at the time of the technological revolution that enabled farmers to move from subsistence crops to surplus. At that time, everyone from artisan to teacher, entertainer to toolmaker, was able to attempt to sell services and wares to those with excess food to barter (or vice versa). Presumably, however, from the time of humans living in organized groups, there was a dynamic of "sales" taking place as tribe members and clansmen attempted to convince their comrades to follow a certain type of prey, go to war, create a new campsite, or elect them their leader.

Humans have been selling something, including themselves, for quite a long time. Moreover, "sales training" has been one of the most abiding, ubiquitous, and popular human development needs in corporate America for the entire time I've been in consulting, and that is now approaching 30 years.

All of us sell something at some time: to our organizations, our customers, our civic groups, our social sets, our professional affiliations, our networks, and our family (the last sell being the toughest). Consequently, it's important for virtually anyone who ever intends to try to influence anyone else to learn something about the art of the sale.

The Three Requisites for Successful Selling

My observation is that truly outstanding salespeople—that is, those who can consistently sell to others on a win/win basis over prolonged periods—operate in an optimal dynamic. And that dynamic has three components, as shown in Figure 1-1:

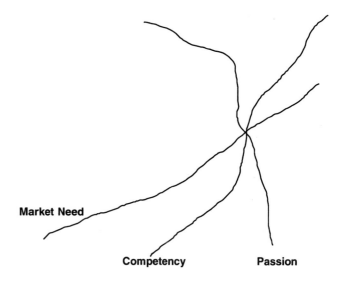

Figure 1-1: The dynamics of the optimal sales environment

1. Market Need

There must be a market need for what you're selling. That need may already exist, or you may create it. No one knew they had a "need" for a Walkman™ until Akio Morita, CEO of SONY at the time, created it and suggested that they did. Millions of customers readily agreed.

You can sell briefly into a "needless" market. Temporary fads created opportunities to sell Pet Rocks, Nehru jackets, and dog breath mints. But there must be a perceived need on the part of large numbers of buyers to enable large-scale sales. Some needs are nearly eternal—companies still buy sales skills training because the perceived need to increase sales will never disappear (and you've bought this book for the same reason). Other needs wax and wane: certain investment vehicles, travel destinations, types of cars (convertibles have come roaring back, SUV interest will decline).

Action Items

> Sales Skills 101: The more people perceive a need, the easier to sell your alternative to meet that need. The less people perceive a need, the more you must help them feel that need before you can sell your alternative. Need precedes purchase.

The executive search business fills a fixed need, though the demand may rise and fall depending on availability or resources, the economy, corporate loyalty, and so on. The realty profession is similar. But the consulting profession doesn't have such a readily identifiable need, especially for some of the more ephemeral or exotic subsets. (There is a general agreement on the need for strategy, less so for diversity "management," and less still for customer participation in corporate R&D procedures.)

Market need is created through marketing, branding, positioning, publicity, and a host of other initiatives and tactics.[1] It also arises "spontaneously" from the environmental conditions that exist at any given juncture. Whatever its source, salespeople must have a perceived need to sell into.

2. Competency

The second requisite is the ability to sell. We'll discuss these skills through the remainder of the book, but as an example, these skills (by anybody's definition) would have to include:

- questioning
- articulate speech
- prospect knowledge
- rebutting objections
- building trust
- follow-up

- listening
- product/service knowledge
- industry conversancy
- demonstrating value
- building urgency
- closing

Competencies may be innate or may be acquired. Some of us have "natural" sales skills that we apply without prompting (though it always is better to be consciously competent of what they are so that we can constantly im-

prove them). Others must learn the skills in a more systematic manner.

> Sales Skills 102: Logic makes people think, emotion makes them act. No matter what the product or service, if you can touch the "emotional trigger" of the buyer, the sales will be both accelerated and enhanced. You can easily be too intellectual to make a sale.

However, not all competency is based in skills. Competency is also based in behavior, and behaviors, while modifiable, are not basically "learnable." In other words, in almost every sales situation a good salesperson should be assertive, meaning willing to ask leading questions, willing to rebut objections, anxious to close the sale, and so on. Someone whose comfort zone is essentially nonassertive will have a difficult time making that type of adjustment on a full-time basis.

And if you add the potential need to reduce patience level, increase persuasiveness levels, and make other behavioral modifications from one's "home base," the energy required to sustain such change can result in burnout.

The good news is that the skills aspect of competency can be learned and expanded. The bad news is that the behavior aspect of competency can be modified *but not dramatically altered.* So, are salespeople made or born? Both.

The behaviors needed in most sales positions include:

- high assertiveness
- middle to low patience levels
- calmness under pressure
- flexibility
- high empathy
- high responsiveness

- high persuasiveness
- moderate attention to detail
- decisiveness
- high integrity
- organization
- low sympathy[2]

---

[1]For details on these and other approaches, see my books: *How to Market, Establish a Brand, and Sell Professional Services,* Kennedy Information, 2000, and *How to Establish a Unique Brand in the Consulting Profession,* Jossey-Bass/Pfeiffer, 2001.

[2]Before you write me cards and letters, I'm defining "empathy" as understanding what the other person feels, and "sympathy" as feeling what the other person feels. The former allows you to appreciate and adjust to their position. The latter creates such a bond that the other person "sells you" instead of vice versa. ("You know, you're right, you don't need this product right now.")

Action Items

Sales Stories

Ray was a salesman who used to work for me and who was not selling, despite our constant training and coaching. We were afraid we'd have to let him go.

After nine months, on the verge of termination, Ray hit his stride. He wound up the third highest volume salesman in the company. I asked him what about my brilliant managing had made the difference.

"Oh, it had nothing to do with you," Ray asserted. "I met a sales guy on a plane and, instead of talking about his quota and his commissions, he talked only about his clients and their results. He was totally immersed in his clients' improvement.

"So, I figured that since I was getting fired anyway, I should stop worrying about quotas and talk to prospects about how better off they'd be if they hired us. Guess what? They like to talk about that, and I began to score."

Don't waste training on behavior and passion factors. If you can't become passionate about your customers' improvement, you don't belong in sales. All those successful clothing shops are full of salespeople who insist on finding you that one more perfect accessory, altering the garment so that it fits perfectly, and suggesting color combinations that bring out your best.

If you don't believe that, just try shopping at Nordstrom's, and watch the best retail sales force on earth.

3. Passion

Forget about selling anything, no matter what your competencies and no matter how great the market need, if you don't have passion. And that passion must extend beyond your love for what you're doing. It must embrace the belief that you are convinced that the customer's condition is greatly improved by your intervention.

> Sales Skills 103: The greatest failure of salespeople is to be unconvinced (and, therefore, unconvincing). If you don't believe it, don't do it. The point isn't to "make a sale." The point is to establish a relationship that leads to many sales. Personal belief precedes buyer acceptance.

If you don't believe that, think of people from whom you've purchased a commodity (a car, a computer, a travel package) and those from whom you have not *when all other conditions were roughly equal.* The people with the passion were probably able to establish a better bond, generate more enthusiasm, and provide more excitement or interest than the others. (It's the difference between the car salesperson who immediately says, "Let's go for a test drive!" and the one who demands you make an appointment and, ho hum, we'll get to it.)

Passion also allows you to overcome obstacles more easily, sustain yourself through dry periods, and prospect new markets with more energy. Passion is the most important of the three requisites. I've seen more people fail in sales from lack of passion than either of the other two factors. Consultants, in particular, who are bent on delivery and methodology, and who don't believe they want to get their hands "dirty" in sales, are particularly sad figures. They have passion about what they do, but not passion about actually landing a customer. It's the equivalent of loving food but refusing to learn how to cook or to go to restaurants.

People seldom give you their food.

Sales Challenge #1
(answers at the end of the chapter)

Your prospect is ignoring your well-reasoned arguments and seems to feel no urgency. She tells you that your points are well taken, but that the company uses an outside

Action Items

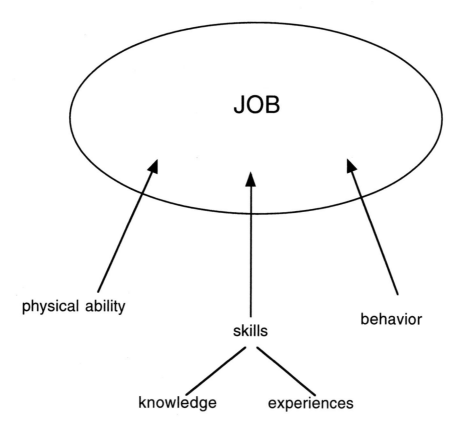

**Figure 1-2: Skills and behavior comprising
a sales position**

firm for its supervisory training needs, and she's sure that they can respond to any future needs in the areas of e-commerce. She doesn't see the need for taking on "still another consulting firm" at the moment, since Web commerce is only 3 percent of her company's revenues at the moment.

She is polite but firm.

Meet the challenge.

The First Sale Is Always to Yourself

You gotta believe. Too many people are trying to sell stuff that they don't honestly believe is right, or that they don't believe they can sell, or that they don't believe they are worth. (After all, in professional services, we're often selling ourselves.)

You must believe that you're worth it. You cannot sell anyone else—pragmatically or ethically—if you don't believe that you are exactly the right person to improve their condition through the product, service, or interven-

tion you are offering. If you don't believe it, why should the buyer?

> Sales Skills 104: Never enter a prospect's presence unless you are absolutely convinced that you have what he or she needs, and that you can significantly improve the prospect's well-being. If you don't believe it, then change your market, change your product, or change your attitude.

There is a "crisis of confidence" among struggling salespeople. In fact, there are major self-esteem issues among those selling themselves. (A great problem here is that even if the sale is somehow consummated, the resultant fee is always too low because the seller "doesn't deserve" a higher fee.) How does one build confidence in the product, service, or relationships being sold?

Action Items

The primary technique is to find out the causes for your past successes. We focus far too much on correcting weakness, and far too little on building on strengths, despite the fact that we truly grow only by building on strengths. Only by finding out why we're good (which is so much more important then merely hearing that we're good) can we replicate and ensure the continuation of that success.

Sales Stories

In the 1970s, I worked for a firm in Princeton, NJ. I gradually rose to become the top officer in North America, and reported to the owner, a genius named Ben. Ben had developed a strategy approach that he sold for $15,000, which was top dollar in the '70s. He would drag me along on the sales calls, since I would often help in the implementation.

At a given juncture during the call, the prospect would inevitably ask, "Well, how much is it?"

Ben always had an unlit cigar in his mouth. He would take it out and say, "Fifteen thousand," and pop the cigar back in. One day I mustered the courage to ask him on the elevator why he insisted on the cigar, and implied that it was somewhat rude.

"That may be," said Ben, "but I need the cigar."

"But why?"

"Because after I say 'fifteen thousand,' if I don't put it back in my mouth, I begin to giggle."

All of us have doubts about our own worth. Get over it.

Find out and build on strengths by:

- Asking people who compliment you why they liked what they saw or heard.

- Making a list of the distinctions that surround your best sales and/or most successful experiences, as compared to others.

- Asking customers, acquaintances, friends, and family what they think your most distinguishing traits and abilities are.

- Undergoing formalized testing.[3]

- Examining your hobbies, interests, and passions for commonalities.

We have to make the toughest sale to ourselves, first. Only then can we generate the conviction and passion that can carry us over prospect objections and obstacles. But we can't climb out of the shadow of our own doubt.

Sales Skills 105: Always understand where you are in your own sales model. That way, you know which small "yes" should be the next target. In this manner, you control the buying dynamic, not the buyer. In every interaction with a true buyer, a sale is made. The critical consideration is that you be the one making it.

Thinking of the Fourth Sale First

I view selling as a process, not an event. There is a series of "small yeses" that lead up to a consummation of goods and services exchanged for some sort of reimbursement. But beyond that "close" there is a project, relationship, and/or series of interventions that may result in a long-term, or even permanent, client.

A former colleague of mine, Mike Robert, called this process "thinking of the fourth sale first." It's as apt a description as any.

---

[3]There are places such as Johnson O'Conner test facilities in major cities that will test everything from verbal ability and rhythm to memory and dexterity.

Action Items

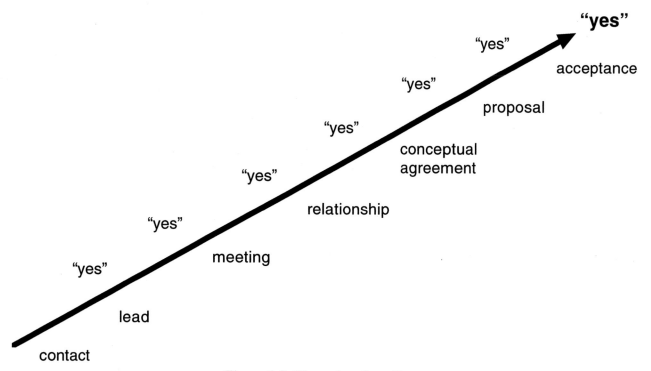

Figure 1-3: The series of small yeses

You may be far better at sales than I, but I have never wandered in to a prospect I have never met and waltzed out with a signed contract. I'll stipulate that, occasionally, such good fortune strikes. But more normally, we have to work a whole lot harder than that. The problem is that we are working hard, but not smart.

The best way to close long-term business relationships is through a series of small yeses at those junctures that constitute your business model. Figure 1-3 shows those junctures in a typical sales business model:

Contact: An introduction to an individual you want to qualify as a lead—someone who can further your prospects in that account.

Lead: Someone who can buy or at least recommend you to a buyer.

Meeting: An opportunity to qualify the economic buyer.

Relationship: A mutual trust with an economic buyer that provides for candid discussion, exploration of the potential to collaborate, and a mutual assessment of the viability of moving forward.

Conceptual agreement: Agreement with the buyer on the objectives (business outcomes) for the project, measures of success to be applied along the way, and

the value of those results to the client organization (which may be a basis for your fees).[4]

Proposal: The willingness of the buyer to accept a proposal based on the conceptual agreement that outlines the details for the project and can be immediately accepted to launch the project.

> Sales Skills 106: If you're discussing price, you've lost control of the discussion. Early discussions should be only about *value*. People may buy based on lowest price, but they engage in long-term relationships over value. Salespeople should have value propositions, not sales propositions or, worse, fee propositions.

Signed proposal: Acceptance and launch.

---

[4]For detailed discussions of the creation of fees based on such value, see my book: *Value-Based Fees: How to Charge for Your Value and Get What You're Worth* (Jossey-Bass/Pfeiffer: 2002).

Action Items

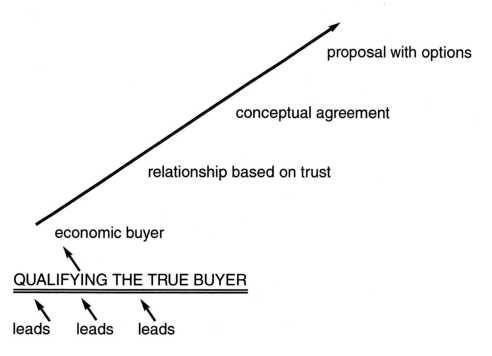

proposal with options

conceptual agreement

relationship based on trust

economic buyer

QUALIFYING THE TRUE BUYER

leads   leads   leads

Figure 1-4: The process of the sale

Your sales model may differ, but the key is always, always to know where you are in your own sales model. Many salespeople are attempting to gain a "yes" when they haven't laid the foundation. (You will have a tough time getting acceptance on a proposal when there is no conceptual agreement. You'll have a hard time gaining conceptual agreement if you haven't built a relationship with an economic buyer.)

Figure 1-4 shows another way to look at the sequence, in which project results reinforce the relationship and, consequently, stimulate continuing and repeat business, referrals, and other business opportunities.

Thinking of the fourth sale first means two things:

1. Gaining acceptance through a series of small yeses, which serve to:

   a. Make the buying process "painless" for the buyer.

   b. Avoid large-scale objections and forge strong relationships.

2. Appreciating the sales process, not the event, so that:

   a. The initial work results in multiple opportunities, not one "close."

   b. Initial project success and results reinforce the relationship with the economic buyer, which, once gained, accelerates all ensuing sales.

Every prospect you ever meet will know pretty well what he or she wants. However, they will seldom know what they *need*. The difference between what they think they want and what they truly need *is your value added.* If you simply respond to a stated want, then you are providing a commodity. Commodities are very sensitive to price competition and "deals." If you are creating and responding to need, you have little or no competition. Price is not the issue, *value is the issue.*

> Sales Skills 107: Always determine "what's in it for her." You know what's in it for you. The idea is to convert your self-interest into the client self-interest, *so that there is a reciprocity of interests.* A "sale" of a training program is strictly in your self-interest. Improved retention rates are in both your self-interests.

If you're concerned about an immediate event, a "close," and a quick first sale, you'll inevitably be responding to "wants" and be subject to price pressure, time pressure, and competitive pressure. But if you're focused on the

Action Items

fourth sale, a sales process, and a buyer relationship, you'll be targeting needs and gaining probability for a long-term client and a series of projects.

Sales Stories

I was introduced to Fred Kerst, Ph.D., one of the most brilliant, hardworking, and ethical leaders I've ever met, when he became CEO of Calgon. Fred was interested in delegation skills because the parent company at the time, Merck, thought it appropriate that Fred was a researcher by training who had come up through the ranks.

As our "small yeses" progressed, I realized that delegation skills were the least of the priorities, since Calgon had been an authoritarian culture in which people did not accept delegation, which wasn't supported by the environment. We both concluded that a more comprehensive approach to the culture and the management team was required, and that one person's delegation skills were a small component of that picture.

I had the pleasure of working with Fred and his team for four years, assisting in the sale of the business to English China Clays and working in almost every facet of the organization along the way. The first sale was delegation skills; the fourth sale was a long-term retainer relationship. The difference was about half a million dollars.

Sales Challenge #2
(answers at the end of the chapter)

Your contact has been cordial and willing to meet several times. He's shared a great deal of company history, culture, and strategy. During your fourth meeting over the course of two months, you're once again unable to elicit objectives for the specific project at hand: improving teamwork among the executive vice president's direct reports.

Your contact urgently requests a proposal, based on everything that you have discussed, and guarantees that it will receive a favorable hearing. You're reluctant to submit a proposal without firm business outcomes, but you've been told the approximate budget and you know it's a lucrative potential contract.

What is your course of action?

Meet the challenge.

How to Find the Other Guy's Self-Interest: Thinking from the Outside In

I use "guy's" here in a colloquial sense, so please don't send cards and letters. But consider the difference in reaction to these two questions:

1. Would you like to see my vacation slides?
2. May I see your vacation slides?

Question #2 is by far much more in the other person's self-interest. Your response is likely to be qualitatively better, with a higher level of commitment, than the response to question #1. People react much more positively to propositions that are phrased to appeal to their self-interest.

Sales Skills 108: When the client says, "I've been rattling on for quite some time," or "We're almost out of time and you really haven't had a chance to say anything," you've been highly successful. You'll never find a prospect sneak a peek at his watch or have her eyes glaze over while the prospect is speaking . . .

Action Items

I call this process "thinking from the outside in." It means that you must accept the responsibility for determining what is in the buyer's self-interest and how best to meet it.[5]

Take a critical look at your sales literature, promotional collateral material, Web site, voice-mail menu, and everything else that constitutes a potential interface with the buyer (or, better yet, have someone else do it for you with a fearless approach). Does it talk about your self-interest, or your prospects'? Here are some red flags or checkpoints to assess your ability to seek out and cater to the buyer's self-interest:

• Is it easy to leave a quick message for you, or must the caller endure endless menu choices and, worse, listen to "commercials" for your services before being allowed to leave word? It seems as if there is an inverse correlation between the size of the firm and the length and complexity of the answering system, as though sole practitioners are compensating for small size with huge phone protocols.

• Does your Web site offer immediate value, or is it an electronic highway billboard? People don't surf the Web to read ads any more than they get in their cars to prowl the roads to read billboards. People visit destinations that offer value. Are you providing techniques, articles, and other resources, or are you simply shouting at people about how good you are?

> Sales Skills 109: Have someone "shop" your own practice and give you feedback. How easy is it to leave a message, obtain information, use your Web site? The answers will inevitably provide direction in "thinking from the outside in."

• Do your brochures talk about client results or about your methodology? Everyone falls in love with their own approaches, but the buyer really cares only about how he or she is better off having dealt with you. Believe me, "the 12-step Questar method of strategy" or "the Jones/Williams teambuilding system" is important only to you and your immediate family, and I'm not so sure about the latter group. Testimonials, client

lists, and examples of results are the three vital elements in convincing prospects that there is something in it for them, because there was obviously something in it for others.

• Are you difficult to get hold of and nonresponsive, or easy to reach and very responsive? I return all of my phone calls within 90 minutes. Do I occasionally, therefore, rush to call back an insurance agent? Sure. But I also demonstrate to prospects that my high level of concern for getting back to them is what they can expect when they become a client. I arrive at meetings on time. I'm "low maintenance" in that I don't need the audio-visual help of George Lucas and Industrial Light and Magic to make a sales call.

• When you converse, do you do most of the talking, or do you ask provocative questions, listen, and keep your mouth shut? You can't learn about someone else's self-interest while you're speaking. Moreover, people most love the sound of their own voice, not yours. As a rule, I like to be speaking with prospects less than 20 percent of the time, and then only in response to direct questions. I know about me, I don't know enough about the other guy.

> Sales Skills 110: If you can't, at any given time, summarize the other person's viewpoint and observations up to that juncture, you just haven't been listening carefully. Summarize mentally as you listen and you'll find that you're considered a great thinker.

Thinking of the fourth sale first and thinking from the outside in are two essential techniques—and philosophies—to build relationships and accelerate your travels along the "succession of yeses." These dynamics are completely controlled by you, not the prospect. They constitute the core competencies in the art of the sale.

Self-assessment

To what extent are you:

• Engaged in areas in which there is market need, for which you have competencies, and about which you have great passion?

---

[5]Note that it's often a waste of time to deal with gatekeepers' self-interests except to do what it takes to get by them to the true economic buyer. Their other self-interests are often in contradiction to the buyer's (safety, low risk, self-glory, and so on).

Action Items

- Self-assured and confident, having made the first sale to yourself, so that low self-esteem is not an extra sales obstacle?

- Thinking of the fourth sale first, building relationships and enduring business rather than "closes," brief events, and one-time sales?

- Thinking from the outside in, so that you can identify the buyer's self-interest and cater to that emotional trigger?

- Establishing needs and not just responding to wants, thereby increasing the perception of your unique value added?

Challenge responses:

#1: You have not created need, so selling an alternative will be fruitless. Retreat and demonstrate why e-commerce will be an essential profit generator, and demonstrate why the buyer's competition is already forging ahead.

#2: You are not talking to a buyer, and your sales model is out of whack. Instead of trying to get business objectives from a gatekeeper, make it a priority to meet the executive vice president who is the real buyer for this team-building project.

Summary of Sales Skills 100

Sales Skills 101: The more people perceive a need, the easier to sell your alternative to meet that need. The less people perceive a need, the more you must help them feel that need before you can sell your alternative. Need precedes purchase.

Sales Skills 102: Logic makes people think, emotion makes them act. No matter what the product or service, if you can touch the "emotional trigger" of the buyer, the sales will be both accelerated and enhanced. You can easily be too intellectual to make a sale.

Sales Skills 103: The greatest failure of salespeople is to be unconvinced (and, therefore, unconvincing). If you don't believe it, don't do it. The point isn't to "make a sale." The point is to establish a relationship that leads to many sales. Personal belief precedes buyer acceptance.

Sales Skills 104: Never enter a prospect's presence unless you are absolutely convinced that you have what he or she needs, and that you can significantly improve the prospect's well-being. If you don't believe it, then change your market, change your product, or change your attitude.

Sales Skills 105: Always understand where you are in your own sales model. That way, you know which small "yes" should be the next target. In this manner, you control the buying dynamic, not the buyer. In every interaction with a true buyer, a sale is made. The critical consideration is that you be the one making it.

Sales Skills 106: If you're discussing price, you've lost control of the discussion. Early discussions should be about only *value*. People may buy based on lowest price, but they engage in long-term relationships over value. Salespeople should have value propositions, not sales propositions or, worse, fee propositions.

Sales Skills 107: Always determine "what's in it for her." You know what's in it for you. The idea is to convert your self-interest into the client self-interest, *so that there is a reciprocity of interests.* A "sale" of a training program is strictly in your self-interest. Improved retention rates are in both your self-interests.

Sales Skills 108: When the client says, "I've been rattling on for quite some time," or "We're almost out of time and you really haven't had a chance to say anything," you've been highly successful. You'll never find a prospect sneak a peek at his watch or have her eyes glaze over while the prospect is speaking . . .

Sales Skills 109: Have someone "shop" your own practice and give you feedback. How easy is it to leave a message, obtain information, use your Web site? The answers will inevitably provide direction in "thinking from the outside in."

Sales Skills 110: If you can't, at any given time, summarize the other person's viewpoint and observations up to that juncture, you just haven't been listening carefully. Summarize mentally as you listen and you'll find that you're considered a great thinker.

Action Items

Chapter 2

Overcoming the Four Resistance Areas

I've heard that one before

If you are active in the sales profession—no matter what your product or service—there comes a point when you've "heard it all before." Early in your career, many objections voiced by prospects are new and novel. One of the disadvantages of being a solo practitioner (or working for a poorly run firm) is that there is no coach or mentor present to help you learn the objections via that person's experience. Unfortunately, you usually must suffer through them yourself.

In any case, there comes a point where you should have heard virtually every objection that can possibly be levied, from "we've just changed our strategy" to "I was abducted by a UFO and the crablike creature warned me not to meet with you again." I am flabbergasted by anyone who has been in their chosen profession for more than a couple of years and still encounters objections that they can't counter.

Don't misunderstand: Not every objection can be overcome, but every one of them can be countered, rebutted, and refuted. You might not win that battle, but at least you can throw a punch. It's absurd to be blindsided or to say, "Whoa—I didn't see that one coming!" If you agree with the premise in Chapter 1, that selling began at about the time subsistence farming ended several centuries ago, then it's logical to conclude that every objection imaginable has been created, recycled, and regurgitated ever since. ("We don't understand technology here" and "We don't do business overseas" are just modern variants of "We can't take telephone orders" and "We don't think there's a need for this type of pottery in Babylonia," just like "My e-mail must have gotten lost" is the electronic equivalent of "The dog ate my homework.")

To make matters even simpler, there are basically four areas of resistance within which objections arise. Consequently, developing expertise in preventing and battling the four major types of resistance will enable you to more readily counter specific objections raised within them.

> Sales Skills 201: There is nothing new under the sales sun, and that includes buyers' objections to whatever it is you're selling. Unfortunately, most sales professionals concentrate on emphasizing features and benefits rather than responding to specific buyer objections. The former are for you; the latter are for the person who can sign your check.

The Four Basic Areas of Sales Resistance

The four basic areas of resistance are:

1. No trust. The buyer does not feel comfortable with you, and consequently prefers not to travel onward. The buyer is reluctant to share his or her true objectives, private and confidential information, past experiences, and so on. Or, even worse, the buyer tells you what you want to hear or innocuous information just to keep you at arm's length. *Most of the inability to make progress during the sales process is due to no trust, although salespeople believe it's more likely to be one of the other three areas.*

2. No need. The buyer does not recognize (or place high enough priority on) a need to take action. This usually occurs when you are trying to introduce a new initiative and not repair a current problem, as most buyers will admit to the need to fix something that's causing them grief. But a new computer system, additional insurance, improved time management skills, or a search firm on retainer makes no sense to them because that particular alternative does not seem to address an outstanding need. (You may recall that in Chapter 1 we specified "market need" as a key component for sales success, along with competency and passion.)

Action Items

3. No urgency. The buyer may have a need—or may acknowledge a new one that you create—but feels no hurry in doing anything about it. This most commonly occurs in prospects who are currently doing quite well, so that current, temporary success is covering a multitude of sins. It can also occur when a client has several severe dilemmas, and your particular solution addresses one of relatively low priority. The urgency to fix other things will take precedence. These are frustrating prospects, because you may get complete agreement about the need to do something, but the timing is never right. And it will never be right.

4. No money. The buyer agrees with virtually everything you say but, alas, there simply is no budget. *Most salespeople consider this the most common "objection" and the most difficult to rebut.* However, this area of resistance is merely the most useful to the prospect who is really digging in his heels because of one of the first three. It's simply easier and more final to announce that there is no money *precisely because salespeople are so inept at countering this argument.* It's like an umpire saying "Strike three!" as the batter watches the ball go by. You're out of there, no appeal, end of story. Except that sales is not a game of baseball, and the buyer shouldn't be calling the pitches.

Before we examine how we can deal with these areas of resistance—and, better yet, prevent them—it's important to understand their origin. These aren't arbitrary categories, but are based on a considerable amount of research into and experience about human interactions.

> Sales Skills 202: People will tend to object to change in areas consistent with their social behaviors. That is, you are more likely to get a response of "no money" from an analytic, detailed person than you are from someone who thrives on gaining results, no matter what. Therefore, understanding your buyer's style is a prerequisite to preventing objections.

In the 1930s, a psychologist named William Marsten conducted research into people's basic emotional needs and commensurate behaviors. Through the years the studies were continued in a variety of areas, most notably by Dr. David Merrill in the 1950s and '60s. They were further popularized by Larry Wilson in a number of pragmatic sales courses and training approaches. The best source is a book written by the husband-and-wife team of Robert and Dorothy Grover Bolton, *Social Style/Management Style: Developing Productive Work Relationships* (AMACOM, 1984). (There have been several works that have usurped and copied these ideas without any attribution at all. They are trivial and unimportant.)

The approach evolved into the presentation of different styles using a simple double-axis chart:

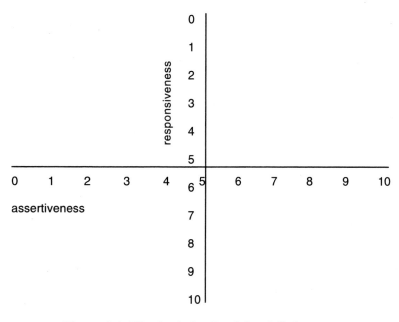

Figure 2-1: The basis for "social style" theory

Action Items

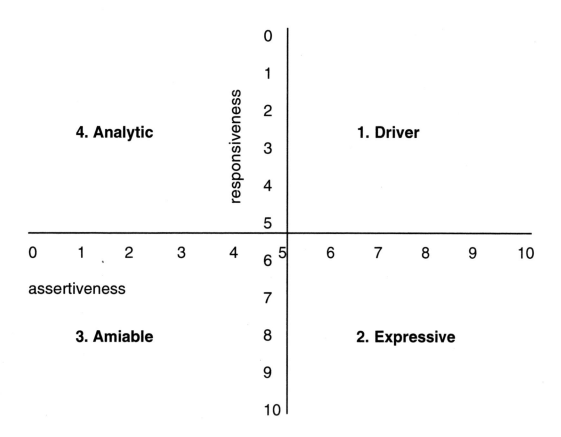

Figure 2-2: The social styles

The horizontal line represents one's assertiveness in most circumstances. Although we all have the capability of movement and change, we also all have a "comfort zone" or "home base," which is our usual level of assertiveness. There are no value judgments: Low assertiveness (reactive more than proactive, tendencies to listen rather than lead) can be as effective as high assertiveness (high goal orientation, act now and make corrections along the way rather than wait).

The vertical line is responsiveness, or social initiative. It represents, on the low end, stoicism, a "poker face," and the ability to work with people, but not the requirement to work with people in order to feel fulfilled. On the high end, responsiveness manifests itself in obvious body language and nonverbal behavior, a need to lead others and work with a team, and a desire to be recognized.

The research has shown that about 25 percent of the general population—regardless of gender, origin, and other factors—falls into each of the four quadrants, as shown in Figure 2-2.

> Sales Skills 203: One's style is always valid. Don't make value judgments, and don't mistake the descriptors for "labels." The idea is not to "explain away" behavior, but to try to understand it so that you can anticipate problems and exploit strengths.

1. The "driver"

This individual wants to get things done. Do not waste time. He or she can work with others if that's required to reach a goal, but working with others is simply a means, not an end. This person is typically motivated by power, since power (freedom of action, resources, control, risk-taking support) is essential to achieving goals. The driver will react to confrontation in an authoritative manner: There is no need to vent or explode (low responsiveness), but there is no inducement to walk away or avoid the con-

Action Items

flict (high assertive). Drivers, of course, can be very intimidating. The key: Let's get it done.

What areas of resistance would you most likely encounter with a driver's style? (Answer below.)

2. The "expressive"

This person shares the driver's high assertiveness, but is also very interactive, socially initiating, and team-oriented. The expressive is motivated by recognition and the limelight. Expressives are natural leaders and motivators, high in enthusiasm and energy. When confronted, they will become highly emotional and even aggressive: They are assertive but also highly responsive. These are the people who may shout, get red in the face, but then forget everything a half hour later. The key: Let's get it done under my leadership.

What areas of resistance would you most likely encounter with an expressive's style?

3. The "amiable"

The amiable style embraces the expressive's high responsiveness and people orientation, but not the assertiveness. Hence, the amiable is a natural follower and team member more than team leader. This person is motivated by acceptance and positive interactions. When confronted, he or she will tend to equivocate, vacillate, or simply acquiesce, because confrontation is anathema (low assertiveness) and cordial relationships are vital (high responsiveness). The key: What are the assurances and guarantees that this will be successful and accepted?

What areas of resistance would you most likely encounter with an amiable's style?

> Sales Skills 204: The four basic social styles will tend to display themselves in a variety of obvious and subtle ways, from choices of language to physical behavior and surroundings. Once you notice a pattern, the key is to adapt to the buyer's style, not to remain resolutely in your own. All of us are capable of such movement around the quadrants, but the buyer has no incentive to do so. You do.

Sales Stories

Organizational culture can often dictate which styles become most successful, and a Darwinian effect takes over. For example, in high-consensus organizations—such as Hewlett-Packard, which has long advocated the "HP Way" of respect and dignity—overconfrontation is discouraged and harmony is emphasized, sometimes to the point of dysfunction or log jam.

I was prospecting a garment manufacturer in the western United States in which five people kept delaying me because each felt that the others would have to approve. "Conversations" were constantly taking place between my visits. I finally demanded a meeting with all of them (two by conference call) and told them I didn't mind if they told me never to return, but I insisted on their reaching some agreement during that hour so we could either move forward to a proposal, or part friends.

To my amazement, they were stunned by the proposal suggestion. "Oh, we don't make the final decision," said a person on the phone, "we just work with the various consultants who come here to make them comfortable with the organization."

I wasn't even dealing with the buyers! They were simply all so polite and wanted so badly to remain cordial, that they didn't want to tell me that the real buyer would never see an outside consultant and that it was very unusual for the organization to ever hire one. They hoped, though, that we could all stay in touch!

Action Items

4. The "analytic"

Also low in assertiveness, like the amiable, the analytic is low in responsiveness, like the driver. This is a person who is an ideal sole contributor, who is happy to work alone, and who immerses himself or herself in detail and objective data. The analytic style is motivated by respect for one's expertise (or else how could anyone become close?—since the analytic is unlikely to reach out, it's important that others make the effort) and will avoid confrontation altogether as impractical and a waste of time. The key: What are the details and do they support the course of action recommended?

What areas of resistance would you most likely encounter with an analytic's style?

Answers to most likely resistance areas:

- Driver: No need
- Expressive: No trust
- Amiable: No urgency
- Analytic: No money

These aren't always, of course, the sole objections, but they do tend to congregate in that way. The driver wants to move quickly, and will rapidly determine whether you can help her. The expressive requires a relationship that will cast him in a favorable light, and relationships demand mutual trust. The amiable needs assurances, so there is no hurry while task forces, committees, and other opinions are solicited (amiables love pilots, drivers hate them). The analytic will look closely at return on investment and existing budgetary constraints (whereas an expressive will more readily exceed the budget in return for credit in leading a new initiative).

A very important disclaimer: This model is provided simply to establish a context for the likely kinds of resistance and *why* they are encountered. It is not meant as "pop psychology," and I caution and admonish everyone to refrain from using labels that restrict our ability to truly understand others. I abhor "Well, what can you expect from a driver?" as much as I do "You can't use an INTJ for that" (a term from the popular Myers-Briggs Type Indicator).

Sales Challenge #3

The prospect is cordial and even effusive, buys you coffee, and sits with you on a comfortable couch in a lavish office overrun with mementos and photographs. After an almost endless discussion about background, hobbies, and family, the buyer simply says, "Let me tell you, I'd love to do business with someone like you, but we have absolutely no money for any outside help."

Then, there is an awkward silence. How do you fill it?

Meet the challenge.

As in most areas of difficulty, it's easier to prevent and avoid problems than it is to encounter and resolve them. However, prevention isn't always possible, and you need good sprinkler systems even though all the electrical connections exceed code and the fire marshal has made the rounds.

Let's examine each of our four areas for prevention and contingencies.

> **Sales Skills 205:** If you know what's likely to happen, there is no excuse for not being prepared. You take an umbrella when you're told to expect rain, and you take along your appropriate arguments and advantages when you know to expect "We don't have the money (or the time, or the need, or the trust)." If you don't, you get soaked—and you deserve it.

No Need: We'd Love to Move Forward, But Why Should We?

"No need" is by far the most common of the objections, not because most prospects are "drivers" but rather because the other styles tend to use various excuses, such as no money, to hide the fact that they really feel no need. They're just more comfortable explaining their resistance using other mechanisms. For example, an amiable would not choose to confront an assertive salesperson by telling him or her that their service simply isn't needed. It's much more comfortable and convenient to say that they need some assurances, will have to get a committee together, and will get back to you.

Relationship-building is the key to avoiding this area of resistance. The more a prospective buyer trusts you, the more that buyer is willing to suspend current biases, re-

Action Items

assess current priorities, and consider the change you're suggesting. It's always difficult to move a buyer from a position of comfort (the status quo) to a position of risk (change). It's easier when the buyer perceives a pressing need, but much harder when the salesperson is trying to create that need.

Build a relationship with a driver by:

- Moving quickly to the point.
- Responding to questions crisply and briefly.
- Never wasting time.
- Demonstrating the outcomes and results in practical terms.
- Being assertive and firmly defending your points.

Build a relationship with an expressive by:

- Sharing personal background and information.
- Asking questions about the buyer's opinions and philosophy.
- Demonstrating how the project will provide clear results.
- Emphasizing the need for leadership and sponsorship.
- Emphasizing the credit and visibility to be gained.

> Sales Skills 206: In the great preponderance of cases, you have to demonstrate need. Not everyone will be as anxious or able to see it as you. The better your relationship, no matter how long it takes to develop, the better the chance that the buyer will be willing to give you the benefit of the doubt.

Build a relationship with an amiable by:

- Providing guarantees and assurances and minimizing risk.
- Being patient and accommodating.
- Demonstrating how to gain acceptance for the idea.
- Providing support in selling the idea, even to subordinates.

- Emphasizing a partnership and collaboration.

Build a relationship with an analytic by:

- Providing careful details, data, facts, and support.
- Respecting the buyer's opinion and incorporating modifications.
- Demonstrating a return on investment.
- Providing metrics and progress indicators.
- Negotiating to protect your interest as well as the buyer's.

In those cases where a buyer sees a need prior to your contact (e.g., customer complaints, lost sales, poor quality, low retention), you still must build the relationship in order to support *the need for your particular solution.* But in those cases where the buyer doesn't feel any pain, relationship building is essential to build both the need for change and the need for your solution.

The more the buyer's style and "comfort zone" is accommodated, the more likely it is that the buyer will listen to previously unconsidered (or even discarded) ideas and suggestions. In other words, you need to win the "benefit of the doubt" before you win the sale.

Sales Stories

When you force people out of their comfort zone, you force yourself out of the sale.

I was meeting with a vice president of human resources at Time Warner in New York who stated an interest to train his staff in consulting skills so that they could better partner with line management. He as an expressive who loves to talk, particularly about his own accomplishments, and who had an altogether unrealistic view of what was needed to gain his goals for the project.

I became impatient with him and his stories and told him that I'd send him a proposal, but that it would be a different

Action Items

approach than he envisioned. He told me subsequently that the fee and the degree of work gave him "an upset stomach."

As a result, I actually sent him Pepto Bismol™ by FedEx™. I won the wise guy award and was chuckling for a while, but to this day Time Warner is not a client. Maybe I simply turned away bad business, but more likely I didn't take the time or have the patience to develop a relationship that would have enabled me to get a fair hearing for the proper way to conduct the project.

No Trust: We Have a Need, But You're Not the One to Fill it

You can view "no need" and "no trust" as being aligned at the hip: Usually, if you resolve one, you resolve the other. What I mean is that relationship-building will gain trust, enabling you to establish need. However, the converse often applies: If you take the time to establish need, you may well have built trust in the process.

But not always. For one thing, need might have been established by some existing business exigency, or by some prior service provider. For another, you may successfully raise issues of need but fail to gain confidence in you or your approach to it.

I define trust in a somewhat different manner for business relationships.

> Trust is the willingness of both buyer and seller to be candid and honest, to share beliefs and opinions, and to be willing to accept at face value the other's willingness to collaborate and create win/win results.

That definition is a mouthful, and the words are not magical or unique. I'm simply stipulating that trust is a function of honest communications and my belief that you're really here to help me (and vice versa). That's why the traditional and stereotypical sales philosophies of "new meat" and "get him to buy three dozen" and "here's another mark" are about win/lose and lack of trust. There is no greater difference than the old auto showroom routine of "I have to take this to my boss and argue on your behalf" and the more common current version of "Let's take a test drive. We sell the car at $1,000 over invoice, and you can verify that on the Internet."

> Sales Skills 207: Once gained and lost, trust is virtually impossible to reacquire. It's shattered when either party abrogates its terms, because each party has invested an emotional component. "You let me down" is one of the most serious accusations that we encounter in business, because it clearly implies that you'll let me down again in the future if you have the chance.

No matter which style you're dealing with, there are constants in establishing and gaining trust.

Ten ways to gain and nurture trust (or conversely, by not doing, to lose it)

1. Meet every commitment and deadline. Don't be late for meetings, with mail, or with deliveries.

2. Look professional in appearance and use professional speech. Dress a little better than the client organization. Never use profanity or make slanderous comments about the competition (yours or theirs).

3. Honor confidences. If you reveal another client's confidential information, you'll be suspected of doing that to the current buyer's organization, as well.

4. Push back. Don't be a "yes person." There are plenty of those in the buyer's own operation. Be willing to tell the buyer that he or she may be wrong.

5. Negotiate only win/win deals. If you want payment in advance, then offer the client a money-back guaran-

Action Items

tee on the quality of your work. Make sure there is a quid pro quo to enrich everyone.

6. Provide references and testimonials. Show the buyer that his or her peers have benefited from working with you.

7. Offer options. There is always more than one way to accomplish an objective. Enable the buyer to make choices so that it's not a question of "your way or no way."

8. Talk casually about prior, nonconfidential client results, and not your methodology or about how good you are. Give examples of success analogous to the buyer's situation.

9. Offer value early and free. You want to create a feeling of "If I'm getting this much value out of initial conversations, how much would I get if I actually hired this person?" Offer suggestions, books, Web sites, and other help on a continuing basis prior to the proposal.

10. Be humble. The chances are that you're not going to solve in 10 minutes a problem the buyer has experienced for 10 months. Also, the buyer must be at least somewhat smart to be in a position of, well, buying. Stress that you're constantly learning yourself and don't claim to have magic answers.

> Sales Skills 208: There is really no such thing as "no time." There is, however, such a thing as "low priority."

No Urgency: We Have a Need and We Trust You, but the Timing's Not Right

Let's get one thing straight: This resistance area is very weak because the timing is never right. No organization ever wakes up and says, "This is an ideal day to change the compensation system," or "The next quarter is perfect for changing our sales process," or "The investment community will really appreciate it if this week we alter our strategy."

We all have all the time we need: 24 hours every day. When a buyer says, "We don't have the time right now," the buyer is actually saying, *I choose not to spend my time on that right now.* These are conscious choices, not a fait accompli.

You can avoid "timing" issues by raising priority issues. That is, you must demonstrate that one of the following conditions will evolve if nothing is done:

- The current problem will become worse and even harder and more expensive to fix.

- The window of opportunity will be lost, and the resultant potential gains will vanish or be minimized.

Time is a nonrenewable resource. You won't do well arguing that your project should get more of it from someone else (especially the buyer). You will get far, however, by demonstrating the *effects* of that lost time. If a prospect believes that a problem is minimal or is disappearing, or that an opportunity is limited and marginally profitable, then your need and solution are lost.

Don't attack the time element, attack the effects. Show that the problem will undermine larger parts of the operation (employee turnover isn't just costing training dollars, but is also damaging client relationships where stability and loyalty are important), or that the opportunity can't be reacquired readily (changing the succession planning process will have positive effects as quickly as next year, when several key executives reach retirement age).

Ironically, the buyer doesn't control urgency. You do. The buyer does control time. So make the debate about something you, and not the buyer, controls.

Sales Challenge #4

The buyer is regaling you with personal stories and successes. You haven't had a chance to get a word in edgewise, much less a conversation about your proposed project to improve the call center's ability to make sales during routine service inquiries.

The buyer pauses after the most recent story and says, "What do you think of that?" How would you respond to get things moving in your direction without moving the buyer out of a comfort zone?

Meet the challenge.

No Money: We Have a Need, Trust You, and Feel the Urgency, but You Can't Do Anything When You Don't Have the Cash

This, of course, is the most frequently heard objection, and the one that forces most salespeople to either fold up

Action Items

their tent or resort to strange discounts and bizarre payment schedules.

Yet it's actually not very formidable at all. "No money" is the resort of someone who has resistance in the other areas, but finds it easier to cite this objection to end the discussions. If you've indeed gained acceptance in the other three areas, then this objection either shouldn't arise or is easily dealt with.

> Sales Skills 209: There is no such thing as "no money." There is always money. The only question is to whom the check is written. In any major organization, in particular, if you accept "no money" or "no budget," you might as well go into another line of work. Sales is not for you.

When a prospect tells me that there is no budget left or no money available for a project, say, to improve management performance evaluations, I always engage in this kind of conversation.

- Let's not worry about budget, let's talk about your return so that we make some reasonable ROI projections. This will save you far more than you spend.

- I appreciate that your budget is expended, but I know that there are other budgets and other interested parties. Who else should we approach?

- Is budget the only thing at this point standing in the way of our proceeding? If we can get the money, would you be willing to sign a contract immediately? If so, let me offer some alternatives to fund this.

- The year is only partly over. What budgeted initiative can be delayed in view of the fact that our project offers a far greater return and produces results that will still benefit that initiative?

- You're spending far more than this right now on failure work, machine warranties, spilled coffee, and ruined postage. Are you telling me that your people and their improvement come after all of that? (See the Sales Stories that follows.)

There is always money. The question is, are you prepared to make an argument that it should be properly invested in you and your project? If you've made diligent progress in the other three areas of resistance, then this one should be easy. When in doubt, just look for a copier machine.

Sales Stories

I was in a New York insurance company that was doing well but having trouble with retention of top producers and the development of future top producers. The senior vice president of sales and I had absolute agreement on the remedy and a fine relationship, except he had receive an unexpected reduction to his budget based on companywide cost-cutting.

"I'm afraid we just have no funds available," he said.

"Is that a Xerox™ machine over there?" I asked idly.

"Yes, do you need a copy of something?"

"How many of those are there in the New York office, do you suppose?"

"I don't know, maybe 100 or 200."

"What would you guess your maintenance contracts are on all those machines, not even counting the postage meters, fax machines, computers, and so on?"

"Well, I'm not . . ."

"I'll tell you what it probably is, somewhere in six figures. Are you really telling me that this company is willing to fund the maintenance of its office machines but won't fund the maintenance and development of its people? What would your board think? What would your CEO think? What would investors think?"

We found the money. To this day I call this the "Xerox Argument."

Action Items

> Sales Skills 210: If you prepare for the four fundamental resistance areas, you should be able to close most sales with most buyers. And the quality and amounts of those sales will be larger than average.

Self-assessment

To what extent are you:

- Identifying your buyers' comfort zones?
- Providing the types of assurances and reactions each style finds most attractive?
- Anticipating and preventing the four major areas of resistance?
- Engaging the buyer in conversation to build trust, need, and urgency?
- Eliminating the validity of "no money" based on other needs?

Challenge responses:

#3: "Let's not talk about money yet. I'd rather gain your agreement on some basic needs and their relative importance. We can always tackle budget in a variety of ways, but only after we're sure that we can really help each other."

#4: "Actually, that brings up a point I've been dying to ask you. What is your philosophy, given your impressive and extensive background, in the need to equip call center people with the skills to make additional sales? My other clients have recorded sales increases of more than 250 percent, but I'm wondering what you've been able to do here . . ."

Summary of Sales Skills 200

Sales Skills 201: There is nothing new under the sales sun, and that includes buyers' objections to whatever it is you're selling. Unfortunately, most sales professionals concentrate on emphasizing features and benefits rather than responding to specific buyer objections. The former are for you; the latter are for the person who can sign your check.

Sales Skills 202: People will tend to object to change in areas consistent with their social behaviors. That is, you are more likely to get a response of "no money" from an analytic, detailed person than you are from someone who thrives on gaining results, no matter what. Therefore, understanding your buyer's style is a prerequisite to preventing objections.

Sales Skills 203: One's style is always valid. Don't make value judgments, and don't mistake the descriptors for "labels." The idea is not to "explain away" behavior, but to try to understand it so that you can anticipate problems and exploit strengths.

Sales Skills 204: The four basic social styles will tend to display themselves in a variety of obvious and subtle ways, from choices of language to physical behavior and surroundings. Once you notice a pattern, the key is to adapt to the buyer's style, not to remain resolutely in your own. All of us are capable of such movement around the quadrants, but the buyer has no incentive to do so. You do.

Sales Skills 205: If you know what's likely to happen, there is no excuse for not being prepared. You take an umbrella when you're told to expect rain, and you take along your appropriate arguments and advantages when you know to expect "We don't have the money (or the time, or the need, or the trust)." If you don't, you get soaked—and you deserve it.

Sales Skills 206: In the great preponderance of cases, you have to demonstrate need. Not everyone will be as anxious or able to see it as you. The better your relationship, no matter how long it takes to develop, the better the chance that the buyer will be willing to give you the benefit of the doubt.

Sales Skills 207: Once gained and lost, trust is virtually impossible to reacquire. It's shattered when either party abrogates its terms, because each party has invested an emotional component. "You let me down" is one of the most serious accusations that we encounter in business, because it clearly implies that you'll let me down again in the future if you have the chance.

Sales Skills 208: There is really no such thing as "no time." There is, however, such a thing as "low priority."

Sales Skills 209: There is no such thing as "no money." There is always money. The only question is to whom the check is written. In any major organization, in particular, if you accept "no money" or "no budget," you might as well go into another line of work. Sales is not for you.

Sales Skills 210: If you prepare for the four fundamental resistance areas, you should be able to close most sales with most buyers. And the quality and amounts of those sales will be larger than average.

Action Items

Chapter 3

Creating Unique Value Propositions

What have you done for me lately?

The problem with sales is that there are too many people selling things. There are not nearly enough people creating value for the client. If you heed no other lesson in this book, heed that one, because the people doing the latter are setting themselves apart from the crowd.

I'm constantly asked, "How do I differentiate myself from everyone else?" Unfortunately, most people's answer to that question is to add more features and benefits, bells and whistles, meat and potatoes. The buyer has to work in order to translate those inputs into outcomes—in other words, "What's in it for me?" That's a question every buyer has a right to ask.

I bought this neat ratchet wrench once, "The Wonder Wrench," from a television infomercial I just couldn't resist. The idea was to love The Wonder Wrench so much that you would go on to purchase The Wonder Drill, The Wonder Sander, and so on. And The Wonder Wrench did come with a terrific carrying case (for distant wrench jobs), a modernistic handle, and a large variety of sockets and stuff. You could also use it with one hand (so that you could eat lunch or change your car's oil with your other one). The trouble was, the configuration of the business end of the wrench prevented me from using it in tight corners, which is precisely the areas where there happen to be a lot of nuts to tighten.

The Wonder Wrench had great features but lousy results. Consequently, it had no value, and no further Wonder Tools were purchased. The ROI for me was effectively zero.

Are you trying to sell pretty tools that don't actually help the client build anything?

Defining Your Value in Terms of Business Outcomes

One of the reasons I've long maintained that we are all in businesses that require intellectual breadth is that we must be able to translate our experiences and competencies into *business outcomes for the buyer.* The "What's in it for me?" question can be answered only by a tightened bolt,

not a futuristic handle or an on-line instruction guide. And since logic helps people to think, but emotion motivates them to act, *finding an emotional outcome is an even more important aspect of defining value.*

If you think back to our discussion about social style, drivers are motivated by power, expressives by recognition, amiables by acceptance, and analytics by respect for their expertise. The more such factors can be interwoven into the buying proposition, the better.

> Sales Skills 301: Your value is important only in terms of a buyer's perceived outcomes. The "things that you do" at best have a temporary appeal. It's the "things that you produce" that linger after your departure, that have permanence in terms of value for the buyer.

Hertz (and its competitors) tried to create differentiation with frequent renter features. Inducements such as the "#1 Club"™ and gold service helped to avoid the airport lines, but still wound up forcing customers to wait for a crowded bus and sit through several more terminal stops before reaching the rental car area. Other features, such as a car already warmed up with motor on, the trunk open awaiting baggage, and computerized driving directions all added bells and whistles, but still there was that bus.

The highest Hertz program, Platinum, is little known and not open to application. Only the very best customers are invited, and it means pickup and delivery at the airport curb—no bus, ever. That's a tremendous value to me— saved time, no waiting in the elements, no dealing with crowds on a bus, no hauling of luggage—and I'm forever loyal to Hertz. All of the prior added features were really no different from Avis's and others', and none was really that important as long as that dreaded wait and bus ride were in store for me.

Action Items

Consultant's Past	Competency/Methodology	Client's Future
• Experiences	• Observation	• Larger Sales
• Education	• Workshops	• Higher Retention
• Victories and Defeats	• Facilitation	• Lower Attrition
• Travel	• Coaching	• Reduced Stress
• Socialization	• Manuals	• Better Communication
• Collaborations	• Training	• Faster Responsiveness
• Socialization	• Focus Groups	• Larger Market Share
• Problem Solving	• Systems and Procedures	• Enhanced Image
• Decision Making	• Conflict Resolution	• Greater Safety
• Planning	• Negotiating	• Higher Quality
• Innovation	• Confrontation	• Reduced Expenses
• Etc.	• Etc.	• Etc.
Consultant raw material	Consultant transfer mechanism	Client results

Figure 3-1: The consultant's past translated into the client's future

Adding "things" to your sale doesn't help; adding results accelerates the sale.

The real business we're in is the transfer of our past and our experiences, via our competencies and abilities, into the client's future. Look at it as presented in Figure 3-1.

The problem with most sales professionals is that they place their emphasis on (and, worse, base their fees on) the first two columns in Figure 3-1. They either stress their own backgrounds:

- I've worked in your industry
- I've faced problems such as yours
- Here is my client list
- This is what I accomplished

or they stress their technology and transfer mechanisms:

- Look at the testimonials on the quality of my instruction
- We have a unique sales training and monitoring system

- We are certified coaches
- We offer a trademarked system

instead of highlighting the client's outcomes:

- Your public image will be enhanced
- Sales closing time will be reduced by at least a third
- Customer response time will be halved
- Your team will stop having turf battles in meetings

> Sales Skills 302: The only person qualified and possessing the requisite knowledge to translate your unique background into the client's desired future is you. If you don't take pains to do this, *no one else is capable of or interested in doing it.* Why keep the secret?

Action Items

Input	Output
• Sales training program	• Improved sales
• Employee survey	• Improved communications
• Retainer search services	• Candidates immediately available
• On-line viewing guide	• Selection made in your office
• Strategy retreat	• New corporate direction
• "Here are my testimonials"	• "Here's what you can achieve"
• Keynote speech	• Create conference enthusiasm
• Focus groups	• Assess weakness in compensation
• Observe the operation	• Identify potential cost reductions
• Improve teamwork	• End divisive turf battles

Figure 3-2: Examples of "conversion" from input to output

In your conversations, in your brochures, on your Web site, in your collateral materials, you must convert your own input into the buyer's output. Yet almost all "marketing material" I see can glaze my eyes over talking about how good the seller is and not what's in it for me. Take a look at your print, electronic, and related materials, and test them for a results orientation.

Figure 3-2 offers some examples of the "conversion" to output from input.

Unique value propositions and marketplace differentiation are not a matter of increasing what we offer. They are a matter of increasing what the buyer perceives as lasting improvement.

Sales Stories

I was searching for a car for my wife for Valentine's Day. She had to make the final decision (a car is too important and personal to make an error about), but I was to narrow down the choices. A Jaguar seemed ideal.

After looking at the sedans, the salesman suggested I sit in the convertible.

"We already have a convertible," I pointed out.

"Well, just sit in it to see what it feels like," he suggested. It felt, well, fabulous. "How about a test drive, just because you have the chance?" he said, and it was a pretty appealing idea.

The car was terrific. When we returned he said, "Now, I want you to drive the supercharged model, since you like fast cars."

"Well, okay," I said, "but my wife would never go for the performance model."

"Hey, you're already here," he intelligently pointed out. The supercharged convertible was just great.

When I brought my wife in, she liked the convertibles, and drove the regular model. Then the salesman brought her to a group of them in various colors, to choose.

"That black one on the end," she said,

Action Items

> "is prettier. It looks slightly different from the rest."
>
> "Oh," said the salesman innocently, "that's the supercharged version that your husband also drove. It does look much sportier than the others, and buyers have told me that it feels different and makes them feel—I know it's silly—but younger."
>
> We left with the high performance convertible. It didn't matter to me that we already had a convertible, and it didn't matter to my wife that the engine was 370 horsepower and supercharged. But you know, the car does drive wonderfully, and you do feel a lot younger . . .

Demonstrating Tangible Measures of Improvement

Once you've cast your approach in terms of client outcomes, it's useful to enable the buyer to understand how you'll both recognize the results (or, at least, progress toward those results). The "gap" between the purchase, acceptance, or launch of a project is often far too removed from the intended result or outcome. Buyers deserve (and amiables will usually insist upon) some progress points along the way. This is particularly true when the results require substantial time before significant results can be seen, for example, increased sales, improved community perception, better succession planning, and so on.

Once a buyer determines that "there's something in it for me," the next logical question is, "How will I know it?" This question *is always important and will always arise sooner or later,* so you can accelerate the sale by dealing with it preemptively and not reactively.

One of the great land mines here is that *the wrong thing is measured,* providing temporary information but not long-term satisfaction. One of the great, daily, stereotypical examples occurs in the world of training, a basic endeavor in any organization. But let's not forget that the purpose of training is to produce some result on the job that we can measure and appreciate. If training doesn't result in better performance, happier customers, increased profit, and similar salutary effects, then why invest in it?

> Sales Skills 303: Progress points and measures of improvement not only provide comfort for the buyer, but also provide leverage points for the seller to generate more business. This is because the progress points serve as interim demonstrations of success, and you can be a hero prior to the actual completion of the project.

However, in the hands of training and human resource departments, how is training most commonly measured? *By asking the participants.* At the end of most training sessions, the coordinator will diligently require that feedback sheets—"smile sheets" as they're known in the trade—be filled out. The questions will generally include:

- Did the instructor have useful information?
- Did the instructor use visual aids effectively?
- Were the handouts in the same sequence as the presentation?
- Was the room environment comfortable?
- Was there a sufficient variety of food at lunch and breaks?

In fact, participants are the exact worse people to ask about the efficacy of training. For one thing, they are often meant to be provoked and "knocked out" of an existing comfort zone. For another, they haven't had a chance to apply the learning on the job yet. For a third, they will use personal criteria.

> Sales Skills 304: "If you can't measure it, you can't manage it," might be extreme, but "If you can't measure it, you can't convince the buyer you had anything to do with it," is a somewhat more accurate and sobering thought.

The proper people to ask are the participant's immediate superior (what behaviors and results are changed and to what extent) and the customer, if applicable (how the

Action Items

service is improved). There are hundreds of thousands if not millions of training programs with very high smile sheet ratings and virtually no appreciable positive impact on the organization or its customers.

According to the American Society for Training and Development, current expenditures for training alone are in excess of $60 billion annually in the United States alone. But no one knows if that money is well spent, although apparently we are pretty certain about the handouts and food variety.[1]

Sales Challenge #5

The director of human resources keeps insisting that a program you're suggesting be measured by the quantity of the people who go through within a given period. He is paid, he tells you, to "get people trained," and the more trained quickly, the better.

He tells you that once you can guarantee a certain volume of training at an acceptable "per head" price, he will go to the vice president, submit the budget based on your numbers, and you'll be the exclusive training resource company.

What do you do?

Meet the challenge.

I call the metrics we're talking about "measures of success," or "measures of improvement," or even simply "mileposts." They create a dynamic by which the buyer can appreciate the quality and relevance of what you're doing *without having to wait for the actual completion of the project, complete launch, or full delivery.* So, if the objectives are "increased sales," then the measures along the way can include:

- Amount of leads being generated
- Amount of sales calls per week
- Number or proposals submitted
- Average size of new business sales
- Quarterly amount of renewal and repeat business
- Number of referrals per existing account

[1]In fact, most human resources professionals will tell you that there are "four levels" of measurement, based on a simplistic model created by a university professor by the name of Donald Kilpatrick 20 years ago. They are attitude, knowledge learned, behavior change, and job results. Only the final one actually matters, and it's the one that the training community admits it can't really measure well.

- Customer returns or complaints
- Business in new markets generated
- Initial leads converted
- Cost per sale (cost per acquisition)

> Sales Skills 305: The greatest danger in ignoring measures of improvement is that the project is screamingly successful, and the buyer says, "You know, you're a pleasure to work with, but I'm not so sure we wouldn't have accomplished this on our own in any case." At that point, you have effectively been rendered mute and, not incidentally, devoid of repeat business.

Note that the list of measures or progress above contains elements that can be observed daily (leads generated), weekly (amount of sales calls), monthly (customer complaints), and/or quarterly (renewal business). The buyer and you are readily able to determine whether progress is in the right direction, to fine-tune the project, to address and fix problems, and to exploit early successes. The two of you have a dynamic means to manage collaboratively the progress of the project.

This means that you don't have to await the conclusion to look good, and you'll be able to pursue additional business based on progress, not completion. That is a huge advantage for a salesperson, and it's based on your willingness to gain commitment to tangible measures of improvement.

Identifying the Right Buyer

Most sales are not lost because the buyer refuses to budge. Most sales are never even contested because the seller has not found the true buyer. I call the true buyer the "economic buyer" because that is the person who is able to generate a check, pure and simple. Whenever someone says, "I think we're all set, now I have to get approval," he or she is not the economic buyer.

Romancing and seducing anyone other than the economic buyer is like leaving the landing lights on for Amelia Earhart—a nice gesture, but utterly futile.

Action Items

The economic buyer is not readily identifiable by hierarchical position. (Sure, all CEOs or owners are economic buyers, but they probably aren't the right buyer for your selling proposition unless you're dealing with strategy, mergers and acquisition work, and so forth.) Anyone else who is evaluating you, stalling you, or generally making you jump through hoops and balance your briefcase on your nose like a trained seal is a blocker (often called "gatekeepers," although some of them aren't even near the gate).

Economic buyers will vary depending on your products and services, but here's the quickest and best way to find them. Ask yourself these three questions:[2]

1. What is my value added? (See the discussion about value articulated as business outcomes above.)

2. Who, specifically, is likely to write a check for that value?

3. How do I reach those people?

In essence, you've just created a marketing plan, because once you know with some certainty who those people are you also know:

- What they read
- What associations they belong to
- Which sources they tend to listen to
- What professional events they attend
- What their "hot buttons" are
- What pressures they're under
- How they can be best reached and influenced

> Sales Skills 306: Blockers are paid to block you. Economic buyers are paid to get results. The first group is successful when they deny you the opportunity to interact with a true buyer. If you voluntarily spend time with them, you are plotting your own demise.

[2]For an extensive discussion of marketing and how to lure buyers to you, create a brand, etc., see two of my books: *How to Market, Establish a Brand, and Sell Professional Services* (Kennedy Information, 2000), and *How to Establish a Unique Brand in the Consulting Profession* (Jossey-Bass/Pfeiffer, 2001).

In large organizations there may be scores of economic buyers, depending on your services. I've worked with buyers who have six-figure buying capability with titles such as "director of knowledge management" and "manager of international development." The key element is to hit the right target. You can miss a sale as easily by "overshooting" the buyer, and winding up with a high-ranking person who is totally uninterested in your value proposition (no need), as readily as "undershooting" and approaching someone who has no power to buy, no matter how compelling your value proposition.

Sales Stories

I had closed on a postmerger project for what was then GRE Insurance in New York. The project was for $250,000 and was estimated to take about nine months. The payment terms were 50 percent on commencement and 50 percent in 45 days.

With the buyer's oral approval (he was the executive vice president), I began the work even though he had not yet returned the signed proposal (which serves as my contract). However, in a week I did receive a check for $125,000.

After a month there was still no signed contract, yet I did receive the balance of my fee in the next two weeks. I completed the project as planned, and the client and I were both happy with the results. Yet I still didn't have a signed contract.

I finally figured out what was going on. It was easier for that buyer to authorize a quarter of a million dollars in payments to me than it was to get my simple two-and-a-half page proposal through his legal department. He realized that the lawyers would cause endless delays. So, he simply authorized the checks!

Action Items

> Economic buyers find a way to get things done. And I now have a line in my proposals that, in effect, states: "Your check is as good as your signature."

Many times when you're called in to organizations, the titles are deceiving, or the prospect is giving you mixed signals. Here are some questions to ask to help determine whether you're dealing with a true buyer. You don't have to ask them all, and their selection will depend on your personal level of assertiveness and the relationship with the prospect.

Ten questions to determine economic buyers

1. From whose budget will this project be funded?
2. Are you the final (or sole) decision maker?
3. Who initiated the inquiry into this project?
4. Who will be evaluated on the results on the project?
5. With whom do objectives have to be set for this work?
6. Who will be seen as the chief sponsor or champion?
7. Does anyone have veto power over the decision to proceed?
8. Who decided to proceed now, at this time?
9. Who established the urgency and the time frame?
10. If you and I reached agreement and shook hands right now, could we proceed immediately?

> Sales Skills 307: Don't try to find the economic buyer through the criteria of who is evaluating the external resources. That job is often "tasked" to gatekeepers. Instead, find out who is responsible for funding, timing, and results. That person will be your true buyer.

Committees are never economic buyers, because they never have budgets of their own. In 99.9 percent of the cases, committees are simply formalized blockers seeking to evaluate the hired help.

The aspect of finding the true buyer is the essence of successful point-of-contact selling, but it is ignored by the majority of salespeople who would rather get comfortable with who will see them, rather than get uncomfortable seeing the people they should. People in my mentor program regularly cite instances in which "I had the sale made, everything accepted, and then my buyer tells me that he couldn't get approval from his boss." Of course not. Meet the real economic buyer.

You can't expect a gatekeeper to sell your services as effectively as you can. They have too much to lose politically by backing someone their own boss won't accept. And why should their boss accept anyone he or she hasn't met or developed a relationship with?

Sales Challenge #6

You're called one morning by a guy who says, "I've been tasked to find consultants for our sales division. Anyone who is good in sales should be able to sell me over the phone. So, here's your chance: Take five minutes and convince me why we should consider you for our short list of candidates and the next round of interviews in the home office."

What do you say?

Meet the challenge.

Ironically, taking the time at the outset to find the true buyer actually *speeds the sale* once you've found her. In fact, I can make a case that people who are intent on schmoozing the gatekeepers and depending on their largesse are less respected by the economic buyer than those who figure out a way around the blockers. That's because the gatekeepers are subordinates to the buyer, and anyone they recommend and are comfortable with will inevitably be viewed by the buyer as a subordinate *and not as a partner or collaborator.*

In view of these dynamics, the trial by fire for all of us is: Once you've identified the true buyer, how do you avoid, evade, dislodge, and otherwise get through the gatekeepers?

Dealing with Gatekeepers

Let me make my standard disclaimer: Gatekeepers are nice people, have families and pets, don't litter, yada-yada-yada. . . . The only essential point for salespeople is that gatekeepers can hurt you but seldom help you. Oh,

Action Items

occasionally one will provide a key introduction or open a gate, but that's rare and almost always too slow. Much more often, since they can say "no" but can't say "yes," they'll say what they're empowered to say: "NO!"

These folks can hurt you but not help you. Avoid them.

A new person to consulting was in one of my audiences once, and came up to me during a break. "My goodness," he uttered, "I was a gatekeeper! You just described me!"

"Well," I said, "then you should have an inside track on how to get around people like you in your new profession!" With that thought he smiled and went back to his notes.

> Sales Skills 308: Your job is about closing business, not making people like you or being overly concerned with everyone's feelings. If you are consumed with everyone liking you, then stand on the street corner and give away money. But if you're concerned about acquiring customers and clients, then don't be afraid to charge past a gatekeeper. You can always break down, scale, burrow under, or otherwise circumvent any gate.

There are three primary ways to deal with gatekeepers. We'll examine them in their most desirable priorities. All of these assume that you've determined the person you're dealing with is not the economic buyer, and you are resolved to meet the economic buyer.

Technique #1: Invite collaboration through enlightened self-interest

If you can rapidly enlist the gatekeeper to your cause and commit to introduce you to the economic buyer, everyone wins. However, this must be done quickly. If it requires four visits or 19 e-mails or other preconditions, you're just being delayed and deceived.

To develop a "win/win" mentality on the part of the gatekeeper, try these arguments and approaches:

- It's unfair for the gatekeeper to be your marketing person. You should take the risks, not the gatekeeper.

- The two of you represent the "virtual team" that can carry the project forward (and thereby share credit).

- You both need to hear from the buyer's lips what his or her expectations are, to determine whether you are, indeed, right for the job.

- You cannot (and will not) submit a proposal until you understand the buyer's needs and your ability to meet them.

- Remember the various social styles. Gatekeepers, too, will want detail, or guarantees, or recognition, or power. In my experience, few gatekeepers are drivers. If they were, they wouldn't be gatekeepers for someone else. You may have to force the gatekeeper out of his or her comfort zone for you to be effective. (Otherwise, you take weeks assuring an amiable, playing to the ego of an expressive, or providing data for an analytic, none of which has anything to do with the true buyer, whose comfort zone you should respect.)

Sales Stories

Fleet Bank's Private Clients Group recommended that I listen to two financial planners. Since Fleet has had a terrific relationship with me, I agreed. My wife and I sat with them around a table in our home.

The investment guy spoke for 45 minutes, using charts and tables, showing us how we could save our kids a million dollars in estate taxes by buying expensive insurance policies today. He occasionally asked me a question, and was responsive to my own questions. He never looked at my wife, not did he elicit anything from her.

At the 45-minute mark, my wife suddenly said, "At that point in your chart, when our kids have saved one million or so, how old are they?"

"Uh, let's see," he said, "they're 52."

Action Items

> "You want us to spend money today that we could be spending to enjoy while we're together with our kids in order to save them a million dollars when they're nearly our age? I don't think so. By that time, they'll be more than comfortable and should be able to take care of themselves."
>
> That was it, meeting awkwardly over. The financial guy never bothered to find out who the real economic buyer was.

> Sales Skills 309: It is sometimes uncomfortable and disquieting to upset a gatekeeper. Of course, that pain is nothing compared to not getting the business or, worse, wasting months of your time before not getting the business. If gatekeepers stop you, you are using the wrong tactics, under the wrong impression, or in the wrong business.

Technique #2: Applying guile

If rational self-interest doesn't work, then it's time for some feints, tricks, and illusions. I call this guile, because you've got to come up with some plausible excuse to get the gate open.

My favorites are these:

- For ethical reasons, I must see the person from whose budget I will be paid to ensure that we are agreed on expectations. I'm happy to work with you on implementation, but I'm sure you can appreciate that I must operate in that fashion. (The word "ethics" usually gets even a hardened gatekeeper thinking.)

- In my experience, I've been burned before—and so has my internal partner—when the budget owner

states that we weren't really accomplishing what he wanted. You and I have to avoid that at all costs, and the only way to do it is with a meeting and a written summary.

- I can't base a proposal on anything other than a meeting with the sponsor of the project. I know you've tried to faithfully relay her sentiments, but I don't want you or me to look bad if either one of us uses a wrong interpretation.

- I have to examine possible conflicts of interest, non-compete potential, and other legal and procedural issues. It won't take long, but we can't proceed until I'm sure that you're safe and I'm safe.

Guile will often work. The key here is to present a greater risk in not opening the gate than in opening it and ushering you in.

Technique #3: Brute force

If techniques #1 and #2 don't work, then simply blow up the gatekeeper. Don't worry about hurt feelings and retribution: *You aren't going to get the business anyway, so no risk here can be excessive. Go for it.*

The techniques for simply brushing aside the gatekeeper include:

- Send a letter, e-mail, or fax to the true buyer and say, "I've had a wonderful briefing from your assistant, but at this point I can't submit a proposal without hearing some things from you directly. It would only require a brief meeting, but it is essential for the quality of our project. When may I see you at your convenience?" Remember, you can't lose anything by asking, because there is no introduction otherwise forthcoming.

- Manage to "run into" the buyer at the cafeteria, outside a meeting room, or in the parking lost. Mention who you are, praise the gatekeeper, and ask if you can get a few minutes of time.

- Find a third party to introduce you. This may be another company employee or someone on the outside. Establish an alternative route.

Don't disparage the gatekeeper, but don't play his game. You need to get inside and out of the elements.

Action Items

> Sales Skills 310: Gatekeepers are empowered and enabled by docility. It is, literally, either them or you. It is more than a little ironic to expect to make a sale to an economic buyer but be waylaid by a gatekeeper. Try to convince them quickly of the need to meet the buyer but, failing that, blast through. They are not called "impenetrable fortress keepers."

Self-assessment

To what extent are you:

- Defining your value as a business outcome for the buyer?
- Translating inputs (tasks) into outputs (results)?
- Providing tangible measures of progress?
- Identifying and reaching the true buyer?
- Effectively eliminating gatekeepers?

Challenge Responses

#5: Tell him that, while you're quite happy to provide favorable fees in return for an exclusive contract, you've seen too many of these questioned—and many an internal career ruined—by an executive who later says, "What did we get for this investment, anyway?" Tell him that you both need to safeguard against that by ensuring that the person with the budget get his or her personal expectations fulfilled in a measurable and tangible manner. You are not dealing with a buyer yet.

#6: You say, "Here's my expertise in sales: This is a relationship business, and I wouldn't insult you or your company by trying to do a soft-shoe over the phone. I assume you're testing for that kind of integrity and sophistication. I am happy to come to your company and meet the person making the decision, however. Do you want to compare calendars?"

Summary of Sales Skills 300

Sales Skills 301: Your value is important only in terms of a buyer's perceived outcomes. The "things that you do" at best have a temporary appeal. It's the "things that you produce" that linger after your departure, that have permanence in terms of value for the buyer.

Sales Skills 302: The only person qualified and possessing the requisite knowledge to translate your unique background into the client's desired future is you. If you don't take pains to do this, *no one else is capable of or interested in doing it.* Why keep the secret?

Sales Skills 303: Progress points and measures of improvement not only provide comfort for the buyer, but also provide leverage points for the seller to generate more business. This is because the progress points serve as interim demonstrations of success, and you can be a hero prior to the actual completion of the project.

Sales Skills 304: "If you can't measure it, you can't manage it," might be extreme, but "If you can't measure it, you can't convince the buyer you had anything to do with it," is a somewhat more accurate and sobering thought.

Sales Skills 305: The greatest danger in ignoring measures of improvement is that the project is screamingly successful, and the buyer says, "You know, you're a pleasure to work with, but I'm not so sure we wouldn't have accomplished this on our own in any case." At that point, you have effectively been rendered mute and, not incidentally, devoid of repeat business.

Sales Skills 306: Blockers are paid to block you. Economic buyers are paid to get results. The first group is successful when they deny you the opportunity to interact with a true buyer. If you voluntarily spend time with them, you are plotting your own demise.

Sales Skills 307: Don't try to find the economic buyer through the criteria of who is evaluating the external resources. That job is often "tasked" to gatekeepers. Instead, find out who is responsible for funding, timing, and results. That person will be your true buyer.

Sales Skills 308: Your job is about closing business, not making people like you or being overly concerned with everyone's feelings. If you are consumed with everyone liking you, then stand on the street corner and give away money. But if you're concerned about acquiring customers and clients, then don't be afraid to charge past a gatekeeper. You can always break down, scale, burrow under, or otherwise circumvent any gate.

Action Items

Sales Skills 309: It is sometimes uncomfortable and disquieting to upset a gatekeeper. Of course, that pain is nothing compared to not getting the business or, worse, wasting months of your time before not getting the business. If gatekeepers stop you, you are using the wrong tactics, under the wrong impression, or in the wrong business.

Sales Skills 310: Gatekeepers are empowered and enabled by docility. It is, literally, either them or you. It is more than a little ironic to expect to make a sale to an economic buyer but be waylaid by a gatekeeper. Try to convince them quickly of the need to meet the buyer but, failing that, blast through. They are not called "impenetrable fortress keepers."

Action Items

Chapter 4

Reversing Objections

I'm not leaving, because you need me

We've established that there is nothing new under the sales sun: If you're new to the sales profession, you'll have heard every objection there is to hear within six months or less—and the more active you are, the faster the learning. If you're a veteran in the profession, you've already heard it all before.

Therefore, it's a crime for anyone with even minimal experience to be surprised by a buyer's objections. However, being able to listen to them without experiencing cardiac arrest is just the threshold of dealing with them. The true professional should know *how to reverse* any objection. Think of it as the judo of selling—using the other person's own momentum to help you gain the advantage.

We talked earlier about finding emotional triggers, and that logic makes people *think* but emotion makes them *act*. Emotionally, there is a thin line between love and hate, resistance and acceptance, rejection and commitment. That's because, when the emotional content is high, it remains high even when one is converted to the counterargument.

There's an old aphorism that says, "There is no zealot like the converted." In other words, no one musters the same amount of passion, commitment, and energy for a cause as someone who initially opposed it with that same degree of passion, commitment, and energy! While it sounds like a bizarre phenomenon, it's really not: Passion drives people strongly on either side of an issue. Thus, the key is to garner their passion while you convert it to your side of the issue.

Figure 4-1 shows that "open doors" exist to convert a client's passion and momentum to your position, creating a common position. The key is how to apply the correct techniques to alter the client's direction while using the buyer's existing emotion and inertia.

> Sales Skills 401: Buyer volume, objection, and vocal resistance are *positives*. If the buyer didn't care at all, he or she wouldn't bother to protest so vehemently. Temporary issues may separate you, but common passion is sufficient to unite positions if you can find the right opportunity and use the right techniques to make this happen during the relationship-building process.

Isolating Resistance to an Identifiable Factor

"We don't want to do this," is hardly instructive. "I don't think this will work here because we've never had the freedom to fail as a belief system, so innovation hasn't

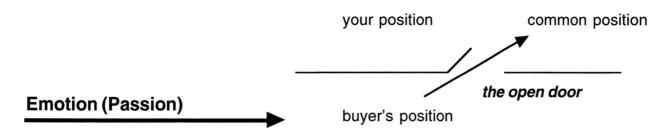

Figure 4-1: Finding the "open door" to convert a buyer's position

Action Items

flourished," is much more useful. The reaction to the first statement can only be "Why?" while the reaction to the second statement can be "Would you be willing to spend 20 minutes with me to learn how we could overcome the fear of failure, culturally, within 90 days?"

The more amorphous the resistance, the more difficult it is to counter. Try eating soup with a fork. You get the barest flavor, but no substance. The more detailed the resistance, the more specific your ability to counter and convert. The movement toward isolation of the resistance is the job of the salesperson, not the buyer.

Sales Stories

I once saw a motivational speaker who enchanted an audience, and then spent the final 20 minutes of his allotted time hawking his audio-tape album. It was $395, and he concluded with a mighty challenge.

"I defy any of you to give me one good reason why you can't buy this album, right now, right here. Not one of you has any reason not to!"

With that, a man in the back held up his hand and said, "I just can't afford it. What better excuse is there?"

The speaker didn't lose a beat:

"Are you a high school graduate, sir?"

"I am."

"How long have you been out of high school?"

"Eight years."

"Have you been steadily employed for those eight years?"

"Yes, with the same company, and promoted twice."

"Well sir, **that's exactly why you must buy my tapes.** If you're a high school

graduate steadily employed for eight years and you **can't afford** to spend $395, then you desperately need what I've got to tell you!"

The speaker was surrounded by people waving cash and credit cards, including the original protester. I've never seen such an effective judo move in so short a time period.

Some people have called therapy the process of taking a generalized unease and turning it into specific, stark-raving fear. Countering objections is not dissimilar (and no less noble work). Help the prospect to understand *exactly* what it is that's causing his or her resistance to your help. Here's an example:

Buyer: We don't think we're in a position to look for a new home right now. We know we need one with the growing family, but the timing isn't right.

Seller: Is it the roots you have to this community?

Buyer: Oh, no, we moved here five years ago and our families are on the other coast.

Seller: Is it a question of a second job?

Buyer: I stopped working when our second child was born, and my husband can easily work from the areas we'd like to live in some day.

Seller: Is it the down payment?

Buyer: Well, frankly, that is our big headache. We can support the mortgage payments on an even more expensive home, but our disposable funds are tied up.

Seller: If I found a way for you to qualify for only a 10 percent down payment, would that take care of your concern?

Buyer: Well, I suppose so. Can that be done?

Seller: I'm not promising anything yet, but for me to proceed just confirm for me: If I can find a 10 percent down payment option, there is no other obstacle and we can pursue a new home immediately. Is that right?

Action Items

In plumbing for the true resistance, you can constantly ask these types of questions:[1]

- If we eliminate this, is there anything else in our way?

- If I satisfy this (or guarantee it) can we move forward?

- What is prohibiting you from acting right now?

- If you and I find a way to resolve that single issue, can we reach a final agreement?

- I'm hearing that there's really one impediment to our work together, and it's XXXX. If I can come back to you tomorrow with XXXX eliminated, would you sign the agreement?

If the buyer says, "No," then find out what else is acting as a resistance issue. If the buyer says, "Yes," then reaffirm the agreement to move forward with the change required, and get to work on it.

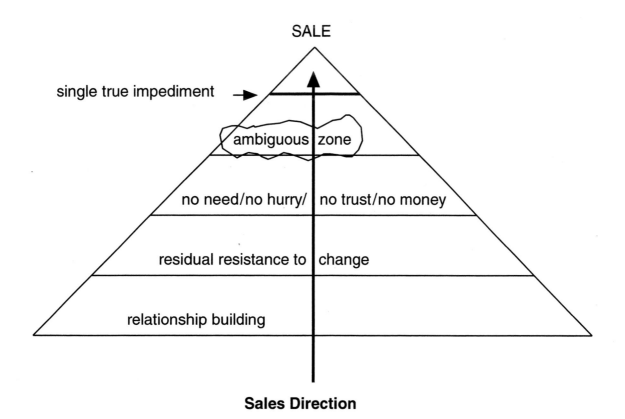

Figure 4-2: Moving to, and through, the single true impediment

[1]All of these techniques assume that you're talking to the economic buyer.

Action Items

Using Turnaround Tactics

One of the most intimidating aspects of sales is running immediately into the "prove it" question. (This typically comes from drivers, but can originate with any style.) The "prove it" takes these forms:

- What can you do for us, exactly?
- How much is this going to cost?
- Why do you think we need someone like you?
- How are you different from all the rest?
- What would be your specific approach?
- How long will this take?
- What would be our return on investment?
- How can I be sure this will work?
- Why should we pay someone else and not do it ourselves?

You get the picture, and you've heard the score. With a figurative finger in your chest, this can be a daunting proposition.

The key, of course, is not to be drawn into the buyer's ballpark (where the equipment, players, rules, home crowd, and even officials all belong to him). The point is to engage the buyer on neutral turf, outside the stadium.

How to do this when you've been confronted? Just state the obvious: "I don't know." The only problem that emerges occurs when you try to imply that you *do* know!

When a buyer says to me, "What do you do?" I respond, "I improve individual and organizational effectiveness." The buyer then says (as I've anticipated), "Well, that's pretty vague, how do you do that?" Now I've got him where I want him.

"Well, it is pretty vague," I admit, "and I don't want to waste your time, so I'll tell you what—tell me something about your organization and your needs, and then I'll respond more specifically in terms of your situation." No one has ever refused that request, first because it's reasonable, and second because most people love to hear themselves talk about—well—themselves.

When buyer says, "How much?" I say, "I don't know, because I don't know what you need. Why don't we begin with that, and then I can provide your options and investment alternatives?" How can you turn that down?

I can take virtually any imperative, demanding, high volume, or otherwise intimidating question and rip the underpinnings right out of it by admitting that I can't answer it *while implying that I'll be able to if the questioner provides a little information.* That's the essence of what I call a turnaround tactic: You use the energy and power of the question to turn it around with equal velocity and acceleration, sort of like sending a satellite around a planet to gain momentum from its gravitational field.

> Sales Skills 404: Never feel compelled to respond to a question just because it's authoritative (the hallmark of drivers) or loud. And never step into silences, however awkward they are. You'll always—ALWAYS—say something you'll regret, and if it's at all about fees, you'll usually rue the day.

In fact, you're doing a great service to the buyer, since you really *can't* know if you can help, how you can help, what it will take, or how much it will cost until you know the landscape and the expectations. Turnaround tactics are actually in the buyer's self-interest. You have to exert the discipline and the fortitude to use them effectively.

Sales Challenge #7

The buyer says, "We've done this project every two or three years, the parameters are clear, and the same consultant helped us every time, so we have a clear view of how this works. She has a conflict this time, and we're looking for a replacement. Since we have a model in place, can you tell us quickly how much you would charge and how long you would take? We're asking everyone the same questions so that we can make a quick decision."

What would you reply?

Meet the challenge.

If you ever have the feeling that you're "cornered" or being driven into a conversation that you'd rather not be having, you're stuck on the buyer's field of play. Moreover, if you find yourself talking about fee early in any relationship, you've lost control of the conversation. Discussions should be only about value, never about fee. And value

Action Items

can be discussed only in terms of business outcomes and the buyer's expectations. Those issues simply can't be addressed if you're responding to questions, doing all the talking, and constantly backpedaling.

One final point about turnaround tactics: It is especially important that you don't reinforce the wrong behavior. If you react like a trained seal to every demand that the buyer makes, then even if you get the business, the demands will never stop. The more you bend over backward, the more the buyer will demand that you break your back.

The time to deal with the overbearing—and whether the behavior is due to malice or ignorance doesn't matter—is in the initial sale stages. And you can do this readily by gently applying the "judo" of the turnaround tactic to send the energy back in the other direction.

Adding Information and Other Subtle Tactics to Reverse a "No"

If emotion makes people act, it can also impede them from acting. And there is no emotion as strong as a threatened ego. For example, I've observed that in an interview process, the interviewer is often as afraid of rejection as the interviewee, making the process weak and invalid, since both parties are protecting themselves rather than trying to make bold assessments.

Emotion can act either as a supercharger for the engine, or as the defensive shields on the fictional starship *Enterprise*, helping to deflect and defeat attacks on the ship. In almost every case, the shields outlasted the ammunition and the tactics of the attacker. In the history of warfare, in fact, defensive positions invariably have defeated larger attacking forces (which accounted for most of the carnage in the American Civil War) and most military authorities quote ratios in the range of three-to-one to six-to-one to carry an entrenched position with a frontal attack.

Fortunately, sales is not war and sales relationships need not be adversarial. But even with the best of preparation and the sharpest of tactics, the buyer will sometimes simply say "no." (And sometimes, you haven't prepared well or used the best tactics—we all have our bad days—and the client easily says "no.")

Action Items

The key point to remember is that "no" doesn't mean "never," and a "no" is never final. How many times have you reversed yourself? Here are just some of the issues that I had been *firmly entrenched against* and that I've happily changed. I said I would never:

- Own a timeshare
- Play pool in a smoky bar
- Eat an oyster
- Smoke a cigar
- Drink scotch
- Drive across country
- Go to an opera
- Ski
- Work with a partner
- Have a colonoscopy
- Drive a convertible
- Order from an infomercial

I could go on and on. But with age, maturity, whim, freedom—and often some convincing by a third party—I changed my mind and am happy to have done so. You have your own list. We all change our abject opposition, no matter how deeply felt, in the face of changing times and better arguments to the contrary.

> Sales Skills 406: Don't be depressed by a "no." Simply regard it as any other objection and use the techniques designed to change it. You'll need an emotional trigger to bring the buyer at least back to neutral. That's easier— and safer—than going from "drive" to "reverse" without an intermediate stop.

Here are some techniques to change a "no" to neutral, and eventually to a "yes." They don't all work every time, but some of them will work for you most of the time.

Add new information

If I've said "no" and you simply want me to change my mind, you've established a bit of a competition, almost an arm-wrestling event. But if you come back to me with *new information,* I can now salve my ego by saying that I hadn't known about that, and why didn't you tell me that before? Here are some examples of new information, and it's sometimes smart to withhold this in preparation for a "no" so that you haven't provided everything all at once.

- I don't think I mentioned our volume discounts.
- Did I point out the free service and extended warranty?

- Did I mention that you can postpone and reschedule without penalty?
- There is a 10 percent discount for full payment on acceptance.
- May I also show you our money-back guarantee?
- I forgot to include that we update for free for the life of the contract.

None of this should sound smarmy or slick, so you have to practice the timing and inflection. The key, remember, isn't to *reverse* the "no," but merely to bring the buyer back to neutral by supplying information that enables the buyer to make that move without loss of face.

> ### Sales Stories
>
> Early in our marriage, my wife and I lived in a high-rise building with a doorman. An encyclopedia salesman had the effrontery to ask the doorman to buzz us without an appointment or any warning. I knew I could handle any door-to-door salesman. I was 25, and I knew all there was to know.
>
> "He has no appointment," I said.
>
> "Well, he says he just wants to drop off your free print. You won it in a random drawing."
>
> "Er, okay, send him up."
>
> The salesman had my free print, which was quite nice, and asked if he might just leave us some literature about the *Britannica.* I said sure, but we didn't need it. He asked why not. I told him that my wife was a teacher, and we had access to all the reference material we needed. (Don't forget, this was well before the Internet.)
>
> He looked at my pregnant wife and said, "Isn't that ironic? Because we provide 10 percent off for a family with

Action Items

children, and I'd be happy to include you on an 'early' basis, and we provide an additional 15 percent off for anyone who is an active teacher. So, while your wife is still on the job, you can save 25 percent."

"I still don't think I can afford the price," I said weakly.

"No problem: Our payment plan allows for just $15 per month, and you don't have to put down a deposit. In fact, if you buy while I'm here, we waive the first 90 days."

I still have those encyclopedias.

Use healthy comparisons

Calmly tell the buyer that his or her peers have usually found the offer very appealing and, since you trust this buyer's judgment and respect his or her position, you'd like to know, for your own education, why the buyer is in the minority.

This technique doesn't challenge the "no" but merely softly informs the buyer that most people have done the exact opposite. When the buyer does provide the rationale, you can then return to your previous discussion and tactics: If that's the only obstacle, and I'm able to remove it or alleviate it, would that be enough to proceed immediately?

Sales Skills 407: Never take it personally. It's almost always not personal. If you disregard your own ego and focus on the buyer's ego, you have a good chance of eventually reversing any objection. If you focus on your own ego and ignore the buyer's ego, you have a good chance of immediately hitting the pavement.

Determine if the resistance is about objectives or alternatives

Conflict is almost always either about the destination or the route to get there. If the buyer agrees with the objective—say, improved closing rates—then focus on that area of agreement, and then provide an entirely new option (e.g., instead of training, suggest coaching and mentoring).

If the conflict is about objectives (e.g., we don't need sales closing to improve, we need better retention of existing clients), then go back to square zero and reestablish the relationship around that point. You've been sailing for the wrong port, no matter how taut your ship, and you need to change course.

Provide options

This is a variation of "new information." Providing alternative delivery, technology, methodology, and/or models might help the buyer find a more appealing route. Sometimes buyers react viscerally to devices they don't trust or have had bad experiences with (e.g., focus groups become gripe sessions).

Also, ask the buyer if the entire approach is unappealing, or if there are elements and aspects that are causing the problem. I've found buyers upset at points as minor as involving their secretary, whom they don't want to share.

Provide phases

Some projects are simply too large for buyers to swallow, or even begin chewing. In that case, break them into bite-size chunks. Create phases, each with mileposts and success indicators, which allow the buyer to more easily digest the plan.

This can be especially useful with amiables who insist on assurance and safety. The key is to make each phase dependent on the former, so that the buyer can't suddenly say, "Enough, we've made sufficient progress!" after only small advances have actually been made.

Action Items

> Sales Skills 408: You may lose a sale (the battle) but you never have to lose a buyer's relationship (the war). The ancient Greeks believed in heroic death, while the Romans believed in living to fight another day. The Romans, of course, thoroughly defeated the Greeks. Do you get my drift?

Living to Fight Another Day

We don't make every sale. Batters don't hit every pitch. Writers don't make every novel a best-seller. Singers don't hit every note. This is why life is so interesting.

Life is about success, not perfection. So are sales.

If you can't reverse all the objections, you can at least stay on good terms with the buyer. Everyone who's been selling for any considerable length of time can cite buyers who have purchased *or referred the salesperson to others who have purchased* even after initial objections and refusals.

There's an old story of a salesman who outsold all others in the company even though located in a remote part of the Midwest with relatively few customers. The home office sent an executive out to watch the guy so that his incredible technique could be replicated throughout the company.

The executive sat in on the first call and found that the salesman opened his catalog to the first page and said to the buyer, "Would you like this?"

The buyer said, "No."

The salesperson turned to the second page of the catalog and said, "Would you like this?"

The buyer said, "No." And so it went on every page through the final page of the catalog. The executive watched in stunned silence. What did the salesman do at this point to get a sale?

The salesman turned the catalog over to page 1 again and said, "Would you like this?"

Perseverance is the basic fuel for inventors, actors, athletes, and salespeople. In many instances, your approach doesn't have to change, but the economy, society, technology, perceptions, ownership, customers, vendors, be-

liefs, law, and/or employees have to change in order to embrace your approach.

A good relationship with an economic buyer is like owning a stock portfolio: You have a valuable asset that you simply haven't cashed in yet. But its value can rise or fall depending on how you manage it. Never allow a "no sale" to create a ruptured relationship.

> Sales Skills 409: The buyers are the roads leading to sales destinations. You might not always reach the destination quickly or on a single road. But if you're smart, you'll invest in keeping the roads well maintained and easily accessible.

Let's conclude this chapter with some tips for maintaining excellent buyer relationships even when the sale isn't imminent: Living to fight another day.

1. Don't take rejection personally. Maintain a peer-level relationship, not one of a supplicant who's been turned down or an adversary who's been defeated. Your ideas didn't fly, but that often happens among colleagues.

2. Thank the buyer for all the time he or she has invested to date. Ask permission, specifically, to approach them again when you have other ideas that may benefit her. Don't simply rely on, "Feel free to call me if you think I can be of help in the future." Establish the fact that you will continue to be in touch.

3. Never bad-mouth or criticize the actual decision. Slandering the competition is very poor form, and critiquing the buyer's firm is just plain stupid. Tell the buyer that you respect the choice, wish him well with it, and say that you are always available as an outside and objective sounding board during the project.[2]

4. Send the buyer something of value now that you know his or her concerns: a book, an article, a tape, a Web site tip, a peer reference—anything that will help the buyer with the current issues.

---

[2]Note that all of this presupposes that you don't simply cease communicating after the buyer says "no" for the final time.

Action Items

Sales Challenge #8

After the proposal is submitted, the buyer simply refuses to return your calls. Despite numerous efforts via phone and e-mail, you can't generate a response, and it's now two weeks past the intended decision date.

The relationship had been good and you're shocked at the nonresponsiveness.

What's your next step?

Meet the challenge.

---

5. If you have a newsletter, electronic or hard copy, include the buyer if he or she is not already on the mailing list.

6. Starting about three months later, let the buyer know by e-mail whenever you're "in the neighborhood," and offer to drop by for a brief chat at the buyer's convenience. If you're smart, you'll plan to be in the neighborhood. This technique works better than half the time, and close to 100 percent of the time if you had to take an airplane to get to the neighborhood.

7. If appropriate, refer business to the buyer. Send someone to his legal firm, to her realty business, to the buyer's retail operation. Have the referrals quote you as the source.

8. Publish some articles (or at least position papers) specifically about the buyer's industry and issues, and send them along with a personal note.

> Sales Skills 410: Your relationship is with the buyer, not the organization. Pursue and follow the buyer. Buyers can take you with them to new conditions and new environments. Organizations usually can't.

9. Study the buyer's company and industry in the trade and business press. As soon as you see an issue you can address, put together something of an emotional appeal and suggest that the two of you get together. I've actually found the buyer's company and sometimes name mentioned, which provides a specific target to hone in on.

10. Remember social occasions. Send out a holiday card. If you know the buyer's son or daughter is graduating on a certain date, send a note of congratulations. Births, grandchildren, anniversaries, and so on are all appropriate for a casual note or card.

Buyers tend to remember good people, even if they can't always do business with them. In many cases, you'll be the recipient of a referral or a surprise phone call that says, "We have a challenge, and I remembered how much I would've liked to work with you last year . . ."

You'll inevitably lose sales, but there's no excuse for losing a buyer.

Self-assessment

To what extent are you:

- Seeking the core resistance and isolating that factor for resolution?

- Employing turnaround tactics?

- Adding information to bring a "no" back to neutral?

- Avoiding being placed on the defensive and resorting to price or fee?

- Maintaining strong buyer relationships even after a "no"?

Challenge responses:

#7: "I appreciate the past work and your comfort. However, I'd like to take just a few minutes to focus on the objectives and goals. Your prior consultant was well immersed in them, which is why she did so well in meeting your needs. So, in order to maximize your results and meet your expectations, let's begin with the results you're seeking to accomplish."

#8: The buyer might be on vacation, in an emergency, or simply embarrassed not to be able to proceed with you. You had a good relationship, so provide the benefit of the doubt. Keep in touch, don't point fingers, and wait to see what occurs. If the buyer is going to abruptly end things, at least don't help with that rupture. (And ask yourself if you missed any signals and were perceiving a better relationship than you actually had.)

Action Items

Summary of Sales Skills 400

Sales Skills 401: Buyer volume, objection, and vocal resistance are *positives*. If the buyer didn't care at all, he or she wouldn't bother to protest so vehemently. Temporary issues may separate you, but common passion is sufficient to unite positions if you can find the right opportunity and use the right techniques to make this happen during the relationship-building process.

Sales Skills 402: Many buyers don't know what their real fear is. They require help to identify and articulate it. In many cases, the fear isn't even real, or can be dealt with easily with a few guarantees. But you won't know this unless you take the time to isolate the true resistance factor.

Sales Skills 403: The "ambiguous zone" can appear anywhere. Never attempt to combat an amorphous mass. Keep driving toward the real barrier. Once you do that, you can convert the buyer's passionate resistance to passionate support.

Sales Skills 404: Never feel compelled to respond to a question just because it's authoritative (the hallmark of drivers) or loud. And never step into silences, however awkward they are. You'll always—ALWAYS—say something you'll regret, and if it's at all about fees, you'll usually rue the day.

Sales Skills 405: Practice turnaround tactics in "safe" situations to become proficient. If someone says, "What do you think you're doing?" reply, "I don't know, what do you think I'm doing?" The defensiveness is immediately removed. Warning: Do not try this with your spouse.

Sales Skills 406: Don't be depressed by a "no." Simply regard it as any other objection and use the techniques designed to change it. You'll need an emotional trigger to bring the buyer at least back to neutral. That's easier—and safer—than going from "drive" to "reverse" without an intermediate stop.

Sales Skills 407: Never take it personally. It's almost always not personal. If you disregard your own ego and focus on the buyer's ego, you have a good chance of eventually reversing any objection. If you focus on your own ego and ignore the buyer's ego, you have a good chance of immediately hitting the pavement.

Sales Skills 408: You may lose a sale (the battle) but you never have to lose a buyer's relationship (the war). The ancient Greeks believed in heroic death, while the Romans believed in living to fight another day. The Romans, of course, thoroughly defeated the Greeks. Do you get my drift?

Sales Skills 409: The buyers are the roads leading to sales destinations. You might not always reach the destination quickly or on a single road. But if you're smart, you'll invest in keeping the roads well maintained and easily accessible.

Sales Skills 410: Your relationship is with the buyer, not the organization. Pursue and follow the buyer. Buyers can take you with them to new conditions and new environments. Organizations usually can't.

Action Items

Chapter 5

Maximizing the Sale

Don't leave your money on the table

One of the great problems in new business acquisition is the phenomenon of leaving money on the table. This means, pure and simple, that there was more revenue and profit to be had, but the seller failed to see it, appreciate it, and/or ask for it. This is a high crime and misdemeanor, since the sales cost has already been absorbed, the heavy lifting has been done, and the client has been sold.

Football commentator John Madden used to lament that a good play wasn't great, because the runner failed to "finish off the run" by gaining the last few available yards. Instead, he went down too quickly, went out of bounds too early, or didn't risk one more hit. Similarly, we have to "finish off" the sale. This is neither mercenary nor greedy, but really a matter of ensuring that the client is deriving maximum use of our talents in return for maximum fees.

Even veteran consultants seem overly eager to take the easy sale and are loathe to jeopardize sure business by pushing the boundaries a bit. But if the relationship is solid and the trust is established, why not press a bit? After all the time and energy invested in reaching a point at which you can close business, why not capitalize on what is the only chance you'll get to do it? Earlier, I advocated "thinking of the fourth sale first." But that doesn't mean that you should shortchange yourself on the initial sale!

I've learned some techniques—usually the hard way, by kicking myself after my omission—to optimize any initial sale. What follows should be easily worth the price of this book.

Providing the Choice of Yeses

The greatest single sales maximizer I know of is the offer of options—what I've come to call "the choice of yeses." The subtle shift from "Should I use Alan?" to "*How* should I use Alan?" is enormous. My unscientific view is that consultants who offer options *every single time, in every proposal* will increase their acceptance level by at least 50 percent and increase their fees by at least 50 percent annually.

> Sales Skills 501: Offering options is a method of involving the buyer in the diagnostic of how to approach the project. Moreover, options induce a buyer to advance up the value chain. You are negligent if you are not including options in every proposal. *Every proposal.*

Options are not phases. The latter are sequential steps, each depending on the prior step's successful completion. The former are *differing ways to achieve the client's stated objectives.* Picture a common destination—say, Nantucket Island. You can go there by ferry, hired boat, commercial plane, or private plane. Or you can go one way and return another. Each has advantages and disadvantages (time, comfort, speed, dependability, etc.). But every one will meet your base objective of arriving at the destination.

The same holds true for client objectives. You can sample employee sentiment to establish a new compensation system by focus group, interviews, mailed surveys, observations, benchmarking comparisons, and so on. You can develop more rapid sales velocity through training, mentoring, different hiring, changes in the reward system, and so forth. I've never been in any client situation, at any time, in any locale, where I couldn't offer options.[1]

Options should be discrete value propositions, each with an increased fee. (I favor going from lowest to highest in the proposal.) Since buyers emotionally believe they get what they pay for—and their own egos are involved in

---

[1]Nor, for that matter, in other environments. If a hotel desk clerk tells me at midnight that my reserved room is no longer available, I remark that I can take a suite (always held for VIPs) at the original rate, be transported to a hotel of equal caliber with expenses paid by this hotel, or wake the general manager to see how that person would handle this. I always get the suite after the desk clerk realizes it's the least painful option for him that will meet my needs.

Action Items

such purchasing decisions—they will seldom choose the least expensive option. They will normally percolate up to the second or third choice. I call this "The Mercedes-Benz Syndrome," meaning that people believe that higher prices denote higher value. In fact, at some point, fee stops trailing value and perceived value starts to trail fee, as seen in Figure 5-1 below.

Options are so powerful that, when you are able to learn the budget for a project, and that budget is ample for your needs, you should nonetheless offer one option above the budgetary limit. If the value is there, clients can find more money, but you won't get it unless you ask. If you don't believe that, think of the times you've purchased non-essential and unplanned sports packages on cars, side trips on vacations, and wardrobe accessories because the value at the point of purchase seemed irresistible. There are a lot of people who own multiple time-share units today who will readily attest to this.

Sales Skills 502: All buyers love to reduce fees, but no buyer wants to reduce value. By escalating your value proposition you'll create irresistible upward pressure on fees. You control this entire dynamic.

The secret to options is to *unbundle* your offerings. Most consultants do the exact opposite: They bundle together everything they possibly can, including the windows and picking up the client's mail, in order to justify what they fear may be too high a fee. Instead, we should all be offering a "bare bones" alternative that will meet the buyer's minimum objectives (we'll get to Nantucket) but also provide additional alternatives to exceed those objectives

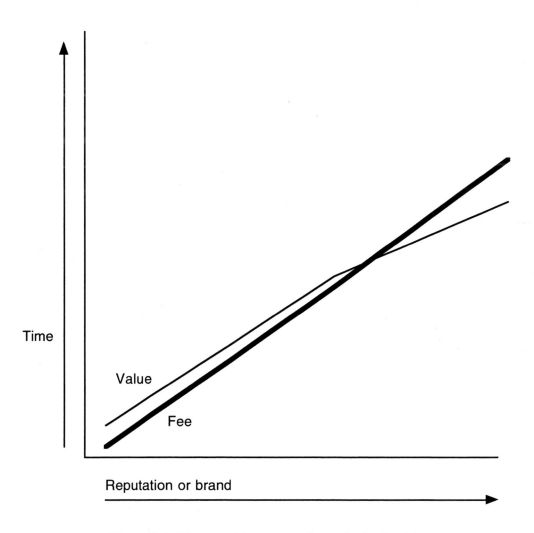

Figure 5-1: The transition from value to fee leadership

Action Items

handsomely (we'll get there with a maximum of comfort, safety, and speed).

Providing options relieves the strain of trying to prove yourself, and instead casts you and the buyer as partners in trying to determine which approach is best for the client. Psychologically, the shift is subtle but extraordinarily powerful.

Here is a quick exercise: Write down everything you're capable of delivering on the left side of a sheet of paper. Then code the entries by color according to the ones that must be partnered or allied. In other words, a needs analysis may be partnered with a decision-making workshop, but probably isn't a required partner for a strategy retreat or conflict resolution session. The similar colors form your various value propositions in a generic manner. Any veteran consultant should have four or five or more. If you find that you're throwing every single item into every single proposal and project for a single fee, well, stop doing that.

Comparisons That Embarrass the Buyer

Many buyers, with heart-wrenching sincerity and tears in their eyes, will tell you between sobs that, much as they would *love* to do business with you, you're just too expensive. Can you possibly reduce your fees, while not sacrificing any value (of course), since this wasn't a budgeted expense and the buyer is going to have to beg in the streets to try to get the fee together in any case.

The fact is, very little consulting work is budgeted at all. The money has to come from somewhere, and clients find the mother lodes: elimination of less important budget items, stepping across departmental boundaries, chargebacks to divisions, slush funds, delayed projects, and a vast array of other kinds of financial mining. You need to confront these protestations very firmly.

I like to do it by embarrassing the client out of them.

As I've noted earlier, I'll often point to the Xerox machine or any other equipment lying about and casually ask how many of them exist in the place. Then I'll ask what the warranties and preventive maintenance entail on all that equipment. *It's always more than the fee for my project,*

Action Items

sometimes more than my highest option. Every sizable organization is spending a fortune on:

- ruined postage
- cafeteria costs
- plants and their upkeep
- physical plant needs

- security services
- coffee and vending machines
- parking lot/garage maintenance
- landscaping

My question is always the same: Is the development of your people (or of your products and services, and so on) really worth that much less than the office plants or the fax machines?

Sales Challenge #9

Your buyer tells you that the budget for the quarter is totally spent, but that you are a "go" for the next quarter, which begins in 60 days. The buyer asks that you be patient until then. He smiles, and is silent.

What's your reply?

Meet the challenge.

People tend to spend more time evaluating their pets' veterinarians than they do their kids' teachers. They are more concerned with the credentials of their tax accountant than those of their doctor. This is human nature. However, it is embarrassing when confronted.

That's what you must do with your buyers who whine about no budget or poor timing. No one sells off the computers or stops providing free coffee. You must help the buyer to recognize what the true priorities are by comparing the power of your alternatives to the mundane expenditures going on all around.

Here are some other sources of potentially painful comparisons:

- competitors
- other industries
- peers
- hierarchical differences

- past history
- other departments
- company expectations
- personal expectations

Sales Skills 504: Some of the most useful comparisons can involve the buyer's own prior expectations. We often find ourselves in worlds of diminished expectations and necessary evils. Sometimes we can help the buyer to rediscover the loftier, more important priorities.

On one occasion, I was debating a proposal with a buyer who was adamant that my least expensive alternative—$65,000—was simply too much because there was no money for such work (improving call center responsiveness) despite a newly discovered realization that customers were deserting. As we talked, a woman slipped into the office without a knock or permission, and proceeded to water several plants in a corner with a large watering can. She quietly left when she was done.

When the buyer paused for a breath, I asked, "Who was that?" He told me she was the plant lady, part of a "highly entrepreneurial" three-person operation. How often are they here—every Wednesday, and all day. After all, there were several hundred plants, and there was watering, fertilization, disease control—and he suddenly caught himself as if a mailbag grabbed by a passing train.

"You're spending far more on the plant people than on the call center people in terms of development," I pointed out. "In a pinch, employees could tend the plants or you could do without them. For exactly how long could you do without the call center people operating at a higher effectiveness and not driving away customers?"

A funny thing happened. I got the job, and the plant people kept theirs, as well.

Sales Stories

I was negotiating a retainer with a rapidly growing dotcom organization selling business-to-business services to other dotcoms. The CFO was a tough negotiator, but I knew he couldn't resist a deal. I cited him a monthly retainer

Action Items

fee for the year, payable quarterly. Sure enough, he began to whittle at it.

"Look," I said, "let's make this simple. I'll give you a full 10 percent off the total if you pay me on January 1." He asked for 15 percent, of course, and we compromised on 12 percent. I picked up a six-figure check during my first visit in January.

Later that year, the company went "poof" and hundreds of dotcoms went under. The client cut back operations, laid people off, and froze hiring. But I was looked on as a key asset, because I was already paid for! I became an even more important resource and the relationship is still strong today.

"Never leave the money on the table" is the *second* most important fee principle. The first is, *always accelerate the payments toward the point where you're paid in full at the outset.*

This is a cash-flow business.

Making timely and astute (and sometimes embarrassing) comparisons can restore the correct perspective to the project you are recommending. Make sure you're armed with as many of them as possible. And keenly look around the environment to identify unique comparisons for any particular client.

You never know who may be watering the plants.

Sales Skills 505: Purchasing agents are paid to conserve funds, remain within budget, and generally reduce expenditures. Why on earth would you want to deal with someone with that responsibility? Line managers and executive are paid to generate results. Don't waste time on the input and cost side when you could be on the output and value side. That's where the big money is.

Avoiding the Purchasing Tar Pit

Several years ago I closed a project with Tom, the general manager of a thriving Hewlett-Packard site. We agreed to begin the project in three weeks, and I told him I'd simply confirm our understanding in a letter of agreement, including objectives, measures, value to HP, and my fees, all of which we had agreed upon in person in his office.

About a week later I received a call from a woman named Margaret, who promptly informed me that she was calling to negotiate my contractual agreement with HP.

"There must be a mistake," I innocently pointed out, "since Tom and I have concluded the agreement."

"Tom," she loftily informed me, "is not empowered to deal with vendors. That's my job."

"I can see the problem," I said, still calm. "I'm not a vendor, I'm a consultant."

"You're a vendor to me," she replied, and the battle was joined.

Margaret told me in no uncertain terms that I was to resubmit my proposal using hourly rates, an estimate of total hours, and that the rates had to compare to or, preferably, be cheaper than, the average of all consulting agreements over the past year. "If you don't do that, and quickly, we don't work with you."

"Fine," I said, "we're not working together." I called Tom and told him we had a problem. His response was absolutely classic: "Alan, do you need more money?"

Well, I thought about that, but then said, "No, it's someone named Margaret," and went on to tell my tale. Tom told me that he had heard rumblings about her, but no one had ever really confronted him with the problem. "I'll take care of it," he said. "Just show up as planned."

Action Items

Margaret was transferred out of the division within the week. I felt no remorse. Her job was to support her line management superiors, not to get in the way with bureaucratic nonsense. I would have walked away from that project if my buyer felt that Margaret had a better handle on the investment in my help than he did. Fortunately for the both of us, he realized that she was an impediment, not a support.

Purchasing agents are paid to conserve budget. They aren't normally familiar with organizational strategy, the outcomes of the project, or the worth of those outcomes to their own organization. And they couldn't care less. At the end of the day, they simply want to prove that they were able to reduce a consultant's fee. I'm not about to help them do that, which means I'm not even about to interact with them. (At least the legal department is concerned with reducing risk and exposure. Those folks will seldom argue about fee, though they will delay things.)

(A brief and important digression, which may be worth a fortune to the reader: So inane and rigid are purchasing department protocols that there is often a *requirement* that any discount extended the organization *must* be accepted. That means—have you guessed?—that even a modest discount for full payment on commencement must be accepted, and you'll get your full fee at the outset. There's nothing quite as rewarding as using ju-jitsu on the bureaucracy.)

> Sales Skills 506: Bureaucratic rules can work both ways. By offering modest inducements, you can actually trigger a Pavlovian purchasing department response to pay you quickly, or make electronic deposits, or pay in advance for expenses. After a while, you stop feeling guilty.

Never allow yourself to be relegated to the purchasing department, not even for "details," "coordination," or "leg work." Remember that their very motivation differs from that of the buyer. The former are evaluated and paid to conserve all expenditures; the latter are evaluated and paid to generate results. The former have a cost orientation; the latter, a value orientation.

For more than a decade, into the '90s, Merck had the leading sales force in the pharmaceutical industry. No matter who you asked, even competitors, the Merck sales force was golden, providing high revenues, fair disclosure, bal-anced presentations, high physician relationships, and so on. They won industry awards for their excellence. Then the health-care landscape changed, and the buying was no longer being done by physicians, but rather by purchasing managers holed up in the basements of places like Kaiser Permanente. These new "buyers" didn't care about the importance of balanced presentations, disclosure of side effects, and trusting relationships. They cared about pennies. And the Merck sales force suddenly became as obsolete and egregiously expensive as the Polish cavalry in an era of trenches, machine guns, and tanks. (Believe it or not, the last Polish cavalry charge actually occurred in World War II.)

You don't want to mount your horse to charge into the roaring artillery of the purchasing people. You want to avoid that battle altogether. They are entrenched defenders, and you are a vulnerable attacker.

Confine your effort to the economic buyer. Refuse, politely but firmly, to deal with functionaries of any sort. Explain any combination of the following (and remember that there are no new objections under the sales sun):

- You and the buyer are partners, and the two of you have to agree on investment and return.

- Your experience is overwhelmingly convincing that the details of the agreement must be approved between the two of you.

- You're willing to work on a "handshake," but that handshake must come from the buyer.

- You'll submit documentation to purchasing only if the buyer provides a clear directive about the terms and conditions to be approved.

- The buyer will not deal with your subordinates, and you don't expect to deal with his for approvals.

- Can the buyer deal with his or her own purchasing department to expedite, since that relationship already exists?

- Purchasing is set up for commodity purchases, not consulting service acquisition.

- The value you're offering the buyer (e.g., unlimited access in return for a capped fee with no "meter running") won't be understood by purchasing.

- Purchasing's insistence on time and materials orientation will result in a more expensive investment than you're now proposing.

- You just don't work that way.

Action Items

Your client is allowed to have policies and so are you. Take the position that you expect the buyer to expedite the conceptual agreement you've both formed, and that purchasing is really his or her problem. If there's a sense of urgency surrounding the project, all the better.

> Sales Skills 507: The way to influence behavior in your favor is to appeal to the other person's rational self-interest. Demonstrate to the buyer that the purchasing department will be a detriment to timing, ROI, expediency, and so on. Place the onus on the buyer to resolve that issue. The probability is strong that the buyer has experienced delays and problems in that area before. Build on that history.

I realize that purchasing is a noble profession, that some of you have best friends who are purchasing managers, and that you've secured sales through purchasing with no problems. I'll stipulate that all of the aforementioned is true. Having done that, let me reemphasize: There is no good that can come from dealing with purchasing, since they will never agree to an *increase* in fees, do not appreciate value or results, and are conditioned and rewarded to pursue *decreases* in fees, regardless of the issues.

Remember Margaret's mantra: "You're a vendor to me."

Sales Stories

I had developed a superb relationship with a buyer over the years, and she had worked with me as a partner on any number of projects. Our work was highly successful and she always looked good as a result.

A particularly difficult project arose, and she asked me to visit—cross country— on my own nickel. I immediately agreed. I provided value and suggested alternative approaches to the extremely delicate project.

At the time, her organization had implemented a rigorous cost-reduction program and both a reduced travel and "no consultants" policy. Yet she was instrumental to a major new initiative and insisted that she could not and would not go forward without my active participation. She needed to involve her superiors for additional budgetary approval, and finally obtained it. I believe I was the sole external consultant hired during the period of cost reduction.

If you demonstrate your value and your partnership, you can overcome almost any barrier or impediment, including "no money," "our policy is against it," and strict cost containment. High value and solid relationships are the armor-piercing bullets that can pierce any defense.

> Sales Skills 508: When all else fails, follow instructions: Find the emotional triggers that will compel the buyer to act. Don't waste time on logic and thinking. There is absolutely no embarrassment in being an "impulse purchase" if the buyer has the impulse—and means—to spend $150,000 on something that means a lot to him.

Playing to the Ego (Emotions Over Logic)

The car salesperson says, "You look cool in that car." The shop owner says, "That dress was made for you." The beautician says, "You have wonderful hair." The captain says, "An excellent wine choice" (even though you chose the Ripple from April—"Much superior to the May vintage, sir"). Excellent salespeople are adept, consciously or unconsciously, at playing to the ego needs of the buyer.

Action Items

Kodak sells "memories," not film. You have to join the "Pepsi generation," not just swill a soda. Women buy Clairol because "they deserve it."

I'm not saying that sales have never been made by appealing to logic and making highly analytic and cerebral arguments. Analytic styles particularly appreciate the detail. But even they have ego needs (e.g., respect, appreciation for their expertise, adherence to a regimen, and so on). What I am suggesting is that these factors are enhanced when emotional needs are met:

- Commitment
- Acceptance of higher fees because of higher perceived value
- Flexibility on terms and compromise
- Loyalty and sponsorship
- Partnering to overcome impediments
- Active enlistment of others and referrals to others
- Acceptance of accountability to overcome organizational blockage
- Repeat business

Sales Challenge #10

Your buyer is in agreement with your oral recommendations for the project. He says, "Submit the proposal to purchasing, it's standard operating procedure. But I'll approve everything and instruct them to proceed. We simply have to make sure we conform with all the rules so as not to create opposition."

Good enough for you? If not, what do you reply?

Meet the challenge.

Here are the questions I've found useful in helping to reach the emotional triggers of the buyer. These are best asked after the relationship-building stage and while the objectives, measures, and value are being established. They needn't all be asked—it would resemble an interrogation—but there's nothing wrong with writing them in our calendar, PDA, or prospect file.

Thirteen Questions to Discover the Buyer's Emotional Needs

1. What does this project mean to you personally?
2. What impact do you seek to have on the organization?
3. What problems did you inherit that you want to remove?
4. How do you want to raise the standards of performance?
5. What influence do you want to have on your customers?
6. How do you want to be viewed by your employees?
7. How will you be evaluated after all is said and done?
8. Why are you doing this now and in this manner?
9. What happens if you fail?
10. Has this ever been accomplished before?
11. Why are you willing to invest in and take prudent risk for this project?
12. What's keeping you up at night?
13. If you could change just one key thing, what would it be?

> Sales Skills 509: Emotional needs will be expressed as a result of trust. Trust is established during the course of relationship-building. Relationships are based on mutual disclosure. Hence, revealing your own emotional triggers will support this process and accelerate it.

One subtle but effective way to plumb your buyer's emotional needs is to reveal your own. I'm not talking about how you were mistreated in your youth or why you never meant to cheat on that history exam. But there are "safe" and relevant disclosures you can make to help the buyer reciprocate. For example:

- "I've found that these projects involve some hard decisions that are often difficult but mandatory."
- "This is a project that would be very challenging, but that I'd love to undertake. Let me tell you why that is."
- "This project has a great personal interest for me because . . ."
- "I began my career on this basis, and I'm happy to have the opportunity to be 'going home' again."

Action Items

- "Let me tell you what my greatest fear is here, and find out if you agree or have different concerns."

If you don't want to leave money on the table, find the emotional trigger; stay out of the purchasing department; make comparisons that embarrass the buyer into proceeding; and provide a "choice of yeses" that shift the decision to *how* the buyer should use you and not *if* the buyer should use you.

The amazing and redeeming aspect of all these tactics is that you control them. If they're not employed, it's because you neglected to do so.

> Sales Skills 510: The seller controls the preponderance of the buying dynamic. How ironic it is that the buyer exerts more influence while controlling the minority of the interaction. Make the best use of your weapons, and your best weapons are offensive, not defensive.

Self-assessment

How well are you:

- Providing a viable set of options (at every point in the sale)?

- Finding comparisons that place your project into a very reasonable perspective?

- Avoiding the purchasing department at all costs?

- Playing to emotions to force both early action and deep commitment?

- Actively managing the majority of the sales dynamic and preparing to do so prior to your discussions?

Challenge Responses:

#9: Demonstrate that the delay will cause more harm, perhaps insurmountable harm. Suggest that you could begin next week on a handshake, and that you'll consider no deposit if the client agrees to full payment on the start of the next quarter. Alternatively point out that there are probably myriad initiatives and investments than can wait an-other quarter without resulting in the harm that this project's delay will produce.

#10: Not good enough. Tell him that your experience strongly suggests that purchasing can unwittingly—and nonmaliciously—delay things. Request that the buyer "walk the proposal down" personally, and get immediate acceptance. Or, can you both talk to the relevant purchasing manager right now on the phone and get that individual's immediate blessing while you're together.

Summary Sales Skills 500

Sales Skills 501: Offering options is a method of involving the buyer in the diagnostic of how to approach the project. Moreover, options induce a buyer to advance up the value chain. You are negligent if you are not including options in every proposal. *Every proposal.*

Sales Skills 502: All buyers love to reduce fees, but no buyer wants to reduce value. By escalating your value proposition you'll create irresistible upward pressure on fees. You control this entire dynamic.

Sales Skills 503: Of course there's "no money." No one awakes in the morning and says, "Let me find a way to budget money for Alan Weiss in case we have need of his services." Moreover, if a client can "find" $50,000, she can find $150,000. Do not go gentle into that good night . . .

Sales Skills 504: Some of the most useful comparisons can involve the buyer's own prior expectations. We often find ourselves in worlds of diminished expectations and necessary evils. Sometimes we can help the buyer to rediscover the loftier, more important priorities.

Sales Skills 505: Purchasing agents are paid to conserve funds, remain within budget, and generally reduce expenditures. Why on earth would you want to deal with someone with that responsibility? Line managers and executives are paid to generate results. Don't waste time on the input and cost side when you could be on the output and value side. That's where the big money is.

Sales Skills 506: Bureaucratic rules can work both ways. By offering modest inducements, you can actually trigger a Pavlovian purchasing department response to pay you quickly, or make electronic deposits, or pay in advance for expenses. After a while, you stop feeling guilty.

Sales Skills 507: The way to influence behavior in your favor is to appeal to the other person's rational self-interest. Demonstrate to the buyer that the purchasing department will be a detriment to timing, ROI, expediency, and so on.

Action Items

Place the onus on the buyer to resolve that issue. The probability is strong that the buyer has experienced delays and problems in that area before. Build on that history.

Sales Skills 508: When all else fails, follow instructions: Find the emotional triggers that will compel the buyer to act. Don't waste time on logic and thinking. There is absolutely no embarrassment in being an "impulse purchase" if the buyer has the impulse—and means—to spend $150,000 on something that means a lot to him.

Sales Skills 509: Emotional needs will be expressed as a result of trust. Trust is established during the course of relationship-building. Relationships are based on mutual disclosure. Hence, revealing your own emotional triggers will support this process and accelerate it.

Sales Skills 510: The seller controls the preponderance of the buying dynamic. How ironic it is that the buyer exerts more influence while controlling the minority of the interaction. Make the best use of your weapons, and your best weapons are offensive, not defensive.

Part II

Expanding Business

Action Items

Chapter 6

The Annuity Factor

I respect you too much for a one-night stand

Everyone knows all the truisms, aphorisms, and exorcisms: It's easier to obtain repeat business than it is to acquire new business. Furthermore, the cost of acquisition is far less, the sales cycle is greatly reduced, and the average size of the sale tends to be larger.

What could make more sense?

In fact, these factors all mitigate toward placing significant emphasis on repeat business acquisition:

- Your credibility is established and suggestions for larger projects will be considered carefully.

- You know the organization well, so there is no re-education required and you can move rapidly.

- Your payment terms and procedures have already been acknowledged and accepted.

- You have met a number of potential buyers and already have at least preliminary relationships built.

- Your prior contacts may well have larger budgets, be prepared to use you again, and/or be in more important positions.

- Your service and delivery personnel can add to top-line sales by identifying and assisting in the development of business in their accounts, which is a very inexpensive method to gain business.

In most professional service organizations, I advocate that between 70 percent and 85 percent of all business should originate with existing customers (and that includes customers and clients who may not have been active continually). The remainder should be the "new blood" that keeps an organization fresh and vibrant, and protected from loss of major customers. However, too many organizations burn themselves out attempting to acquire as much as 90 percent of their business from new sources every year.

That's a recipe for disaster and certainly for low margins. Ironically, the best time to prepare for repeat business acquisition is during the original sale.

> Sales Skills 601: To garner repeat business, you must provide quality work and solid service. But you also have to *ask for it.* Many firms do the first two, and then forget the third.

Setting Up Repeat Business at the First Sale

We discussed earlier the concept of thinking about "the fourth sale first." This is where it pays off.

Your initial sales approach should consider the prospect as a long-term customer, not as a one-time event. Right from the outset, you should be educating your buyer to appreciate the relationship aspects and long-term implications of the mutually beneficial relationship you're suggesting. Here are some "golden" techniques to accomplish that right from the beginning.

Talk about phases: Let the client know that there are several phases or stages that can be tackled, with the initial one taking care of immediate concerns but later ones establishing more ideal conditions. Example: In building a stronger management team, skills transfer of basic competencies (e.g., delegation, conflict resolution, and so on) is Phase 1, but a logical profession would include advanced leadership experiences for Phase 2 (e.g., sophisticated simulations) and, eventually, selected members attending challenging programs (e.g., the Harvard Advance Management Program) as Phase 3. You're the one to plan, evaluate, recommend, and coordinate the progression.

Indicate related factors: There is almost always more than a single factor responsible for problems, critical in planning, or driving innovations. While you might start work on the first, it's important to set the stage for

Action Items

the rest. Example: If sales growth is the target, reducing closing time is certainly a legitimate approach. However, it may also make sense, once that objective is met, to consider cutting the attrition rate and increasing the average amount of the sale.

Demonstrate the gamut of your abilities: Even though you may be discussing a very particular intervention or need, make sure you indicate the complete range of your competencies, to avoid being pigeonholed and not considered for later projects. Example: If the general manager is interested in your assistance with a strategic retreat, mention that you've often served as a coach for people who are called upon to implement the results of such a retreat, since implementation is always the more difficult aspect of strategic work.

Suggest improvements through observation: As a trained observer, you will constantly observe and experience things that can be improved or exploited in your clients. Constructively mention to the client the opportunity for improvement without being self-aggrandizing. Example: If the switchboard constantly puts you on hold or misdirects you, there's a strong possibility that customers are receiving the same treatment. Suggest that the client shop his or her own call system and, if you're right, implement improvements in training, monitoring, and procedures immediately. Volunteer to play a role.

Sales Skills 602: Don't view your role as one of project implementer. See yourself as a partner of the buyer, as interested in and informed about his business as he is. Actively look for and suggest alternatives to improve the client's condition and the buyer's situation. Ask yourself, "What would I do if I were running this place?"

Establish a priority list with the buyer: One of my favorite questions is, "If you could do just three things to improve the operation, what would they be?" Even the most focused buyer will have a list of changes they'd love to accomplish. Conversationally, find out what they are and see if you can successfully raise them as issues to be examined. Example: If the buyer doesn't have the budget for a secondary project to improve call center response, you can suggest that you take a look at the situation while on the current project, offer some insights, and perhaps begin the project modestly this fiscal year. Then you could move more aggressively with the new budget in the next fiscal year. At least you will have begun the process.

Sales Stories

Wandering around a warehouse to gain a full appreciation for my project on resource allocation, I found an old-fashioned pinup calendar on a supervisor's wall. When I told him that the calendar was actually illegal and created a hostile workplace, he told me it was a warehouse, and no one had ever questioned him on it.

When I sought out his manager, I was told the same thing: It's just something that "the boys" do, and no women worked in the area (nor would they, I was slyly told).

I told my buyer, when I reported about how I would attack the staffing issues, that he had a major potential liability in terms of a harassment suit. He listened and said, "I'll call them immediately and read them the riot act."

"That's only part of your problem," I told him, and explained that there was clearly a higher level of awareness about this issue needed at front-line supervisory level, and that the human resources people had been asleep at the switch. Both those issues also needed addressing.

"Can you also help us with that while you're here on the other project?" he asked.

I managed to work it into my calendar and into a second and concurrent project.

Action Items

Reaching Out Laterally

If you accept the fact that an economic buyer is someone who writes a check for your perceived value, then there are scores of them in medium-size organizations, and hundreds in large organizations. There is no protocol that maintains you must speak to only one buyer at a time.

This is not like polygamy.

As you work with your buyer, you will inevitably be introduced to others, sometimes casually in informal meetings and sometimes more formally in cross-functional collaboration. This is the time to take names and begin building relationships.

Many consultants seem to feel that this is somehow too self-aggrandizing, too aggressive, too "sales-oriented." I think that selling is a noble business, if you keep one primary issue in mind: You're reaching out to other buyers because you can help them, not because you're trying to "sell" something.

> Sales Skills 603: Sales is about providing value in return for equitable compensation. If you believe that, then you're negligent in not offering services and products to someone who will be legitimately improved by applying them, and requesting fair recompense for that transfer. If you don't believe that your services can help the buyer, then you have no business selling them.

When you meet other potential economic buyers at a meeting, there's nothing wrong with asking to have lunch, chat on the phone, or stop by their office. The key is to provide them with value—an idea, a suggestion, some feedback. Always keep your current buyer informed, but you can usually make the case that establishing such rapport is actually beneficial for the current project.[1]

For example, I was conducting a major sales analysis for a domestic sales force and, in briefing senior management about the scope of the project, met the vice president in charge of European operations. I chatted casually with him after the meeting, and told him that I suspected many of the findings would apply to Europe as well. He indicated that he'd ask my buyer (his peer) if he could have access to the results.

About two months later, I found myself headed to Europe for another client. I mentioned this to my potential buyer and he agreed it would represent an excellent opportunity to perform some initial interviews since I was going to be near his office sites anyway. Bingo, I had a new client and twice as much business for my European trip. If I hadn't established that prior relationship and raised some early potential, it would have been extremely difficult to make the case at this point.

I had the same opportunity with the head of an R&D division, whom I met at a group lunch one day, and who was fascinated by the succession planning work I was doing for the financial department. I explained how support areas were more common than uncommon, and suggested he talk to my buyer about progress. Since my buyer was delighted, he gave a glowing report. And I suggested that the expenses would be minimized if I could begin some early R&D work during currently scheduled trips, rather than wait until the financial project was completed.

I wound up completing succession planning implementation for every support staff in the division, because eventually no one wanted to be left out.

Sales Challenge #11

You're with a buyer who is considering you for a project, and with whom you've established a preliminary relationship. The buyer says to you, "Look, it's clear from our past efforts in this area that we have to stay focused: The project has to target the improvement of our go-to-market cycle time, and not be distracted. Do you agree or not?"

What's your response, right on the spot?

Meet the challenge.

Another aspect of reaching out laterally pertains to more remote opportunities. For example:

The customer's customers: Clients can be frustrated when their own customers cause them a problem. You can often make the case that the same skills you're imparting to the client ought to be accepted by the customer. Example: Many insurance companies will spend money to educate independent agents, realty chains improve brokers, technology firms develop channel

[1] Of course, you want to retain your current buyer's confidentiality and not disclose anything inappropriate. But that's really not a difficult guideline to observe.

Action Items

partners. Perhaps your work should be extended down the value chain.

The customer's vendors: The auto companies found out quickly that their own stringent quality programs could be completely undermined by less-than-stringent vendors, and began to demand tougher standards from their suppliers. Example: Why shouldn't your quality processes be introduced in your client's vendors to ensure a commonality of quality right from the source?

Sales Skills 604: View your customer as the center of a universe of lateral buying opportunities, then assess which presents you with the best opportunities. Never view any buyer or any client as a singular and narrow experience.

The customer's trade associations: The odds are good that your buyer or her colleagues have served on the board of or are active in several professional trade associations. The membership is a parallel universe to your client. You don't want to imperil the competitive edge, but you can be of general help. Example: Your client can recommend you as a speaker, writer, or advisor to the trade association to help the overall industry. If you help the National Fisheries Institute, you're helping fishing harvesters, processors, restaurants, distributors, and so on—thereby aiding everyone.

As Figure 6-1 demonstrates, there is a considerable potential network of lateral buyers that would constitute the substance of significant expanded and repeat business. This network must be accessed early, even during the pre-proposal relationship-building, if it is to be completely exploited. Creating the type of chart in Figure 6-1 for any new client is an important aspect of rainmaking.

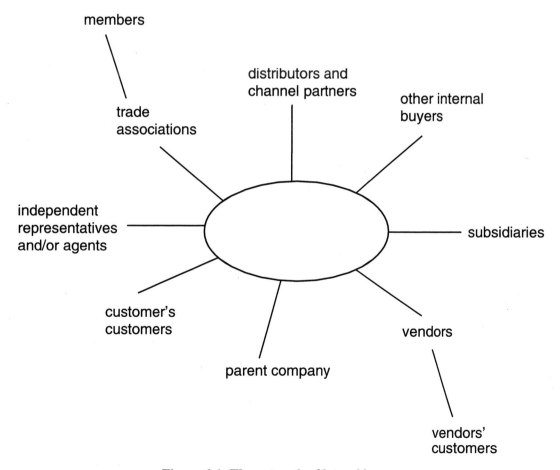

Figure 6-1: The network of lateral buyers

Action Items

Identifying Additional Opportunities

My experience is that consultants don't identify additional opportunity because of their own self-imposed restraints, not because of client unwillingness to listen or buyer skepticism. The key facts to remember about identifying and "selling" against additional opportunities in the course of the engagement are these:

- Emotion, not logic, will encourage action.
- Buyers have egos and pride.
- Your goal is legitimately to further improve the client's condition.
- Your real value is as an outside, objective source of expertise.
- You're running a for-profit business.

Sales Stories

Larry Wilson, the founder of Wilson Learning and one of the most dynamic people I've yet met, told me this story a long time ago.

Wilson lived in Minneapolis, and realizes that his steep driveway needs repaving. Since he's in the sales training business, he's determined not to be taken by a slick sales pitch, and has already estimated that it's about a $300 job.

The guy who owns the paving business is standing at the bottom of the drive with Wilson, who tells him that he just wants a simple repaving job.

"So I shouldn't take out the curve up there, the one that ruins the symmetry of the lawn?" Wilson has never appreciated that, so he tells him to go ahead.

"And the bad depression, where ice could gather, and your wife might lose traction if she doesn't notice?" Wilson has vaguely realized that he's skidded there sometimes, and says to include that.

"I've also noticed that all your neighbors' drives are carefully edged—looks great—but yours is the only one on the block without an edging." Wilson never even had looked at that, and is embarrassed not to have done it.

Once they're in the house to sign the papers, Wilson has agreed to a $3,000 project. The paver says, "Nice house. What line of work are you in?" Wilson says he runs a sales training company.

"Really? Do you think I could get in one of your classes. I could probably use some of that."

"I don't think so," mumbles Wilson.

Emotion, not logic, will encourage action

When you spot additional opportunity, don't attempt to explain it or justify it from your perspective (e.g., "In true teams, there is shared responsibility on a voluntary basis, and we don't have it here"). Instead, demonstrate the issue from the buyer's perspective: "You're not moving ahead on all the projects you're accountable for because your direct reports spend at least half their time arguing over turf and resource issues and you, personally, have to act as referee at least twice a day. Do you agree?"

Action Items

> Sales Skills 606: If you view additional opportunities as things you're "selling" to a buyer, you're creating an adversarial relationship. If you view them, instead, as additional value for the buyer (improvements in his or her condition), then you're creating a partnering relationship. The choice, and the business, is yours.

Don't phrase new issues as consulting challenges or even as parallels to your own experience. Cast them as challenges that either are delaying the buyer's self-interest or are unexploited opportunities that can better achieve that self-interest. Perception is everything.

Buyers have egos and pride

The buyer wants to be told what a great job you're doing, and the better people regard you and your work, the better the buyer looks. ("A great investment" is a far better accolade than "Still another consultant.")

I've never seen any consulting project that exists in isolation. There are always contributing factors, peripheral issues, tangential fallout. As you bring people on board and work with various departments, determine how their goals may be attached to the project. Softly solicit their support for enlarging the scope (and, perhaps, even their investment). Suggest to your buyer that enlarging the original project seems to have broad-based support and that he or she will be seen as the champion and sponsor who helped people across-the-board.

Buyers fear their own initiative and risk-taking being usurped by others as the project they championed (and put themselves and budget on the line for) is obviously successful and others move in to claim credit. Ironically, adding to the project is a way to avoid this for the buyer while also gaining you business.

Your goal is legitimately to further improve the client's condition

I've never suggested any project or approach that wasn't entirely aimed at improving my client. I might have charged handsomely for it, and I may have benefited myself tremendously, but my objective was always my client's well-being.

There's nothing wrong with being paid for that.

As a philosophy, you must embrace and believe that your actions are wholly targeted on that improvement. If you suggest minor side projects, or charge for relatively unimportant assistance, or "nickel and dime" the client on expenses and reimbursements, you won't be viewed as much of a partner. Partners don't do that to each other.

As you observe the operation, use this simple template: Am I seeing something that:

1. Is a major cost or lost opportunity that the client should address in the short term?

2. Has a solution that I can bring to bear or for which I can at least recommend a resource?

3. Has a positive risk/reward component and a strong chance of success?

If those conditions are met, then you'd be negligent if you *didn't* raise the issue with your buyer. After all, there may well come a time when the buyer says, "If you knew about this, how could you keep it to yourself?" That question has no good answer.

> Sales Skills 607: When you don't raise issues, either assuming that the buyer is already aware or fearful of the perception you'll create, you're doing neither the buyer nor yourself a favor. Professional salespeople don't fear sales opportunities. You don't make rain by standing under an umbrella.

Your real value is as an outside, objective source of expertise

Consultants don't make very good "yes men." First of all, that's not why we're hired. But second of all, it does us no good since we're not vying for promotion, have no retirement plan within the client, and don't need a sponsor to get a plum internal perquisite.

The more you demonstrate your value—early—the more chance that you'll not only gain credibility for the current assignment but will also merit first crack at repeat business. That value is readily manifest by identifying and suggesting additional business opportunities for you and

Action Items

the client during the course of the original project. And that's best done by swimming against the tide.

Be a contrarian. Point out that the current turnover rate is not within industry averages and, even if it were, it ought to be reduced. Cite the fact that every person at a meeting is a white male, and that can't be a coincidence. Suggest that the human resource department has no credibility precisely because it's lodged in the legal department and the solution is worse than the problem. You get the idea. Challenge basic premises. Confront the "tried and true."

If you're not doing that—and, worse, unwilling to do that—why do they need you? The client has a plethora of people who won't challenge the status quo as it is.

Sales Challenge #12

Your project requires the support of another department, and the manager there tells you that if your buyer is successful in this project, it makes more work for her area. She can't support the initiative because she doesn't have the resources or the inclination to take on more work. So, the responsiveness you'll need is not going to be forthcoming from her operation—nothing personal of course.

What do you do at this point?

Meet the challenge.

You're running a for-profit business

Finally, let's not lose sight of the fact that consulting is a means to an end: That end is your life, your family, your interests, and so on. Your practice is the economic fuel to run that machinery. If you think consulting is an end unto itself you don't need a client, you need a therapist.

Consequently, you're in this to show a profit. You need a profit mentality. Since it's easier to gain business from an existing client than a prospective client, why take the tough, unpaved road when you've got the car on a super-highway at the moment?

You have to be "hungry" at all times to be an effective hunter. Ask yourself if you'd rather be out prospecting, making "cold calls," or waiting by the telephone rather than suggesting honest and helpful additional projects to your existing client partner. I don't think that's a very tough question to answer.

> Sales Skills 608: Your alternatives are to put your feet on the street, metaphorically, and beat down new doors, or to put your feet up on the client's ottoman and suggest some additional ways for your partner to succeed. Is there really a debate about which is easier, more productive, and more rewarding? You'll get plenty of chances to beat down doors. Why forfeit the chance to help your current partner succeed, and for both of you to profit? We're not talking ethics, we're talking business sense.

"Free" Peripheral Advice

Before we leave the expansion of existing business, I want to comment on a seeming contradiction: You can charge for your work in additional areas of help to the client most easily by originally offering free advice. Before you say this flies in the face of my profit motive, let me explain my rationale and resolve the false contradiction.

You build trust by providing help. The more help, the more trust. The more trust, the more reliance on your advice. The more reliance, the more likelihood that a major project or significant addition will be accepted. That's the cycle you want to create.

> Sales Skills 609: Free advice is not of little value. The client is paying for it, since you've already been engaged. The key is to ensure that the advice can be immediately utilized and the wisdom appreciated.

An example of free advice would be the suggestion that the line operations provide a list of their "musts" for job candidates to the human resources people. They could then screen for the absolute essentials, and the line people could see the "short list" candidates to evaluate desirable ele-

Action Items

ments, chemistry, unique strengths, and so on. That small procedural change would end the finger pointing ("lousy candidates," "no guidance") and would greatly expedite hiring time. It would also provide more quality candidates (and/or demonstrate that the job expectations are incorrect).

That's *a great deal of benefit* from a simple suggestion that would take less than a day to implement in any orga-nization, large or small, public or private, manufacturing or service. (I know, because I've done it dozens of times.) Make two or three of those suggestions—regardless of whether they are related to your current project—and you'll be banking tremendous trust that creates a mu-tual "good deal" for you and the buyer, as expressed in Figure 6-2.

Figure 6-2: The good advice cycle

Sales Stories

In working on a marketing plan for an advertising sales firm, I was pleasantly surprised to find my project expedited by my being able to contact the national salespeople without problem. That's highly unusual, so I began to wonder about it and realized that they were al-ways in their offices when I called.

Upon investigation, I found that they worked in one- or two-person offices in major cities. They were charged, of course, with visiting ad agencies and direct buyers in major organizations. I asked my buyer about their productiv-ity vs. the telemarketers'.

We found that the field sales force was underperforming against both their own plan and their telemarketing counter-parts. I suggested to the client that he could at least save money by having the salespeople work from their homes (no one visited them), but that a field su-pervisory position seemed to make sense despite the travel costs.

The client reassigned a sales manager to outside sales, and call rates, propos-als, and business closes all increased within 60 days. When I suggested a project that would create objective and higher standards for both internal and external sales functions, my proposal was signed within a week.

Action Items

The guidelines for your "free" peripheral advice might include:

- The client can implement quickly.
- The results can be seen short-term.
- There is little cost in the "fix" or opportunity.
- There is little risk—everyone agrees the issue needs improvement.
- The political issues are minor.
- It's clearly your idea and the buyer's initiative.
- There's a measure—objective or subjective—of success.

You might reply, "Well, that's overly restrictive!" but it's not. There are usually procedures (as in my hiring example above), "necessary evils," and general annoyances that everyone wants fixed but no one has been able to view objectively or with "fresh" eyes. Believe me, they abound, due to the very nature of organizational life.

> Sales Skills 610: If you can't generate more business while you're actively partnering with a trusting buyer, then you just aren't trying. Most lost opportunity is due to consultant fear or reluctance, not buyer intransigence. And that is the traditional "good news/bad news."

Begin to create your business annuity when you begin your project, not when you've finished it. You don't create the best retirement plan when you're 60 years old. You create the best plan if you start investing when you're 21.

Self-assessment

How well are you:

- Sensitive to further improvements as you begin a project?
- Reaching out laterally to meet new buyers?
- Creating a "good deal" for your buyer and yourself?
- Confident that you can help the buyer meet emotional needs?
- Offering free advice that becomes trust for major projects?

Challenge Responses:

#11: "Focus is always important, but anything in the extreme is dangerous. In other words, we can't have tunnel vision. I've never seen a major issue such as cycle time that doesn't have multiple forces helping or impeding. We have to take a holistic view if we're not going to fool ourselves and simply put a band-aid on the problem."

#12: "I understand your problem. I'll tell you what: Tell me what, ideally, you'd like to see happen, and I'll go back to my client and discuss what it would take to create a win/win resolution. If I can do that, would you be willing to participate to some extent in that approach?"

Summary of Sales Skills

Sales Skills 601: To garner repeat business, you must provide quality work and solid service. But you also have to *ask for it*. Many firms do the first two, and then forget the third.

Sales Skills 602: Don't view your role as one of project implementer. See yourself as a partner of the buyer, as interested in and informed about his business as he is. Actively look for and suggest alternatives to improve the client's condition and the buyer's situation. Ask yourself, "What would I do if I were running this place?"

Sales Skills 603: Sales is about providing value in return for equitable compensation. If you believe that, then you're negligent in not offering services and products to someone who will be legitimately improved by applying them, and requesting fair recompense for that transfer. If you don't believe that your services can help the buyer, then you have no business selling them.

Sales Skills 604: View your customer as the center of a universe of lateral buying opportunities, then assess which presents you with the best opportunities. Never view any buyer or any client as a singular and narrow experience.

Sales Skills 605: If you're not plotting the totality of the sales potential for ongoing business acquisition right from

Action Items

the outset, then you're not completing your sales accountability. After all the work and expense of business acquisition, why ignore the true business potential?

Sales Skills 606: If you view additional opportunities as things you're "selling" to a buyer, you're creating an adversarial relationship. If you view them, instead, as additional value for the buyer (improvements in his or her condition), then you're creating a partnering relationship. The choice, and the business, is yours.

Sales Skills 607: When you don't raise issues, either assuming that the buyer is already aware or fearful of the perception you'll create, you're doing neither the buyer nor yourself a favor. Professional salespeople don't fear sales opportunities. You don't make rain by standing under an umbrella.

Sales Skills 608: Your alternatives are to put your feet on the street, metaphorically, and beat down new doors, or to put your feet up on the client's ottoman and suggest some additional ways for your partner to succeed. Is there really a debate about which is easier, more productive, and more rewarding? You'll get plenty of chances to beat down doors. Why forfeit the chance to help your current partner succeed, and for both of you to profit? We're not talking ethics, we're talking business sense.

Sales Skills 609: Free advice is not of little value. The client is paying for it, since you've already been engaged. The key is to ensure that the advice can be immediately utilized and the wisdom appreciated.

Sales Skills 610: If you can't generate more business while you're actively partnering with a trusting buyer, then you just aren't trying. Most lost opportunity is due to consultant fear or reluctance, not buyer intransigence. And that is the traditional "good news/bad news."

Action Items

Chapter 7

Solidifying Business

Will you still love me tomorrow?

There was a great '60s song by the Shirelles, titled "Will You Still Love Me Tomorrow?" Every single sales professional reading this book who has built a successful practice or firm or who has starred in a large organization can recall dozens or more clients that suddenly "turned south" without warning.

One day all is sweet and wonderful, and the next day phone calls aren't returned, you're asked to shift gears, you're blamed for client failings, the accolades of the past are conveniently forgotten, and suddenly delays and "rescheduling" become necessary.

You've been dumped.

Like scrambling jet fighters, consultants who have been dumped immediately start pressing every button and making every call imaginable in order to recover. There is a frenzy of activity, but the buttons are no longer connected to anything and the phone calls are unanswered. You're always the last to know!

The key to solidifying business is to *prevent* the circumstances that lead to your being suddenly and summarily fired. This takes more, ironically, than merely good work. It requires the management of an active campaign to safeguard your work and relationships. If that sounds like a theater of war, it is, because to many people you are the opposition, and you're making a long, slow crawl through enemy territory.

After all, if you're not advocating change and threatening the status quo, then why are you there?

The Present Value Discount Principle

I invented the phrase "present value discount principle" as applied to consulting when I tried to determine why it is so hard to dislodge consultants who are already established in clients. Conversely, I wanted to examine how to get myself into that position.

> Sales Skills 701: Make no mistake about it: You face a far greater threat from internal client dynamics and opposition than you ever do from external consulting competition. Yet we are much more alert to and prepared for the latter than the former.

When you begin work with a client, it's important to make yourself as visible, reliable, trustworthy, and *necessary* to the buyer as possible. (Note that you can remain fairly invisible to the organization, if necessary, while still maintaining high visibility with the buyer.) The more you become integral to the buyer's plans, the harder it is to replace you. After a couple of projects and a couple of years, it becomes virtually impossible to replace you from the outside, because any new consultant would have to somehow compensate for your organizational knowledge, connections, experience, acculturation, and so on, despite the attributes that the new consultant may bring.

Even lower fees can't overcome that tremendous value you've created synergistically with the client. The only way that long-established consultants are displaced by newcomers is:

1. They have done something wrong that is so egregious that all past victories are subsumed by the transgression.

2. They have become ineffective because they are offering no new value (same old/same old) or have become the "buyer's mouthpiece" and their recommendations are seen as biased.

3. Organizational opposition has effectively created a "disinformation campaign" to turn the buyer against the consultant.

4. A newcomer brings to the client a dramatically new approach or technology that usurps your position. However, this is really a variant of number 2 above.

Action Items

As with objections (we've heard every one before), we know about these four possible causes for our "ouster." It follows, therefore, that we should be smart enough to do something about them. Here are some suggestions before we examine some very important critical areas.

• *Never surrender the buyer relationship.*

We have a tendency to move away from the buyer toward the implementers after a deal is closed because we love the methodology, prefer implementing to "selling," and are more comfortable with lower-level people. This is almost always a fatal error. It's extremely difficult to regain the buyer's relationship if you abandon it because:

1. You've not created a habit or expectation of meeting.

2. You're now perceived as the peer of subordinates and the buyer's ego will resist a relationship with you.

3. Others have replaced you in reporting on the work and results.

From the outset, you must establish regular, face-to-face meetings with the buyer. Although these may decrease as the project progresses, *if you're not meeting with the buyer at least once a month, you're threatening your future with that client.*

> Sale Skills 702: After the hard work of reaching a buyer and closing business, to abandon that relationship is like climbing Mount Everest and deciding not to look at the view before heading down again. Abandon the peak at your own peril, because most people don't make the climb a second time.

• *Establish relationships with as many key people as possible.*

You will not be accepted by default, and the one thing that works every morning in every business is the grapevine. Meet your buyer's direct reports. Meet the buyer's peers (who are all potential buyers). Meet the "unofficial" leaders (sales stars, respected contributors, union people, and so forth). Don't allow yourself to be derided by indifference.

• *Go the extra mile.*

I've given up the occasional weekend to go to an "emergency" meeting at the client site, filled in for speakers who haven't shown up, missed a flight to make sure a concern was resolved, and spent many an evening at home talking through pressing client issues that would be priorities for the buyer the next morning or were crises from the day before. The more you extend yourself during the unexpected or crucial issues, the more the buyer will extend himself or herself for you.

• *Push back.*

Ironically, the strongest action you can take to invoke the present value discount principle is to resist, rebuke, and reject. Your value will be specifically in *not* being another sycophant surrounding the buyer. You want the buyer to think of you as an objective, prudent, and consistent observer who, although sometimes a royal pain for throwing a wrench into the wheels of a bandwagon charging downhill, always has done so with the buyer's best interests in mind. So long as your objectives are clearly to protect the buyer's plans and position, resisting the popular but imprudent will carve out a very secure niche.

Sales Stories

A client called on a Sunday evening, apologized profusely to my wife, and asked if I might be available. It was the CEO of a $400 million division of an even larger parent client.

He had an impasse between his vice president of sales and vice president of human resources over a field sales practice that the former said was harmless and the latter said was unethical. Both were threatening to resign.

"You have no axe to grind," he said. "Here are the facts. What do you think?"

Then both of us found a common ground, slightly more in favor of the sales position, but requiring some

Action Items

> boundaries to be imposed. The conversation took less than a half hour.
>
> "I can't tell you how much I appreciate your taking the time," he said. I had missed 20 minutes of a drama on television that my wife had captured on tape for me, and I had extended my position in that client by at least another year. In fact, I worked continually for the CEO until he retired, and we're still friends.

Being Perceived as "Part of the Team"

The sales professionals I've seen who were most successful at integrating themselves into the client were some of the field engineers at Calgon Specialty Chemicals in the mid-'90s. The field engineers were actually account representatives, and their job was to acquire and service clients (usually manufacturing plants, utilities, municipal treatment plants, etc.) that needed water treated that was entering and/or leaving the facility.

When I shadowed the best of these people in order to create best practices for everyone else, I found that they shared a common technique that was not written or explained in any handbook, manual, or field procedure.

They had managed to insinuate themselves into internal client teams.

> Sales Skills 703: Team members support each other, establish rapport, suffer common defeats, and rejoice in common victories. A team stands together. If you are a part of such a team, let the momentum sweep you past the rapids and into the deep, blue water.

For example, at one plant there was a team focused on the improvement of standards for wastewater treatment. The group was composed of three client engineers, two operators, one quality control supervisor, and the Calgon

field engineer. They met every other Friday to compare findings, assess their instrument reports, and determine ways to improve the cleansing of the wastewater. Each had specific assignments, and the Calgon guy had the accountability for testing the instruments to ensure accurate recording.

I asked him if he ever became tired of the team, or if it were an infringement on his time. He told me that not only did he like his colleagues, but that they often played softball or went out for beers together, and that it was the easiest way to guarantee repeat business he had ever seen. "I'm almost embarrassed to collect my commissions for this account," he admitted, "but I always manage to cash the check!"

In any business, you should be able to inveigle yourself onto internal task forces, committees, and teams. There are never enough people, more help is always gratefully accepted, and you have to be there anyway in most cases. You can readily be an ex officio member, so that your name doesn't have to appear on reports and therefore no one will question the propriety of your membership. Volunteer for some of the more unpopular duties (e.g., writing summaries or disseminating information between meetings) and/or the ones uniquely suited to an outsider (e.g., benchmarking or assessments of progress).[1]

Sales Challenge #13

The buyer shakes your hand, tells you it's wonderful to be starting the project, that she has high hopes and is always available. Then, she introduces you to her vice president of human resources and administrative assistant and says that they will be your key contacts from here. In fact, the buyer will be traveling for the next month almost constantly.

Are things okay, or do you do something at this point?

Meet the challenge.

An excellent way to be part of the team is to identify, with the buyer, those meetings that are crucial and should always be observed. Many executives have an "executive council" or "executive committee" that meets weekly (or "operations committee" or "strategy group," and so on). By starting even as a silent observer, you can eventually

---

[1]A minor but interesting aspect: Since the team will inevitably have budget constraints, but your travel is paid from your own project's budget, you may actually have more latitude to do things for the team than the internal members.

Action Items

become a contributing member and then an integral part of the group.

Here are some reasons to press on the buyer for your involvement in such meetings and team activities:

- You want to observe the nature of the teamwork and how the various department heads interact.

- You want to observe the leadership style of your buyer with his or her direct reports.

- The meetings will give you an indication of empowerment or disempowerment, teamwork, or mere committee compliance.

- You could serve as an objective facilitator.

- The meeting dynamics might stand improvement, which could suggest that:

- There are too many, too long, and too inefficient meetings, undercutting performance, and you may be able to help consolidate and improve the structure.

- You may have reports from your project that the buyer would like to share "uncensored" with his or her subordinates.

- The meetings serve as a central point for you to gain information and meet with key players at one time.

- You'll serve as the scribe and record key information for your client, which the two of you can later review.

- The meetings are the place for you and the buyer to gain common and uniform understanding of the objectives, metrics, and progress of your project.

You get the idea. Some of these might work better than others in your circumstances, but it is relatively easy to ingratiate yourself and become a member of the team some-

where, at some time. I know that meetings are often the bane of our existence, and should often be shunned. But I'm speaking here of a valuable technique to entrench the present value discount principle: If you're a natural part of the organization's routine, you're less likely to be seen as the expendable "outsider" and more likely to be seen as the valuable "teammate."

Sales Stories

I was able to serve as a special member of a CEO's executive council and was expected at every other biweekly meeting. I had a reporting responsibility, and was urged to contribute during the meetings. I received all preparatory materials and notes. (Of course, I had signed nondisclosure agreements.)

During this process, I was able to become closely acquainted with the 10 top vice presidents, from manufacturing to operations, from finance to sales. Two of them asked me to engage in separate projects for them, and one of the others called me a year later after he had moved to another firm and needed help there.

The only delicate aspect was at times when I felt my buyer's position was wrong and needed refuting. Since many people in the room were reluctant to do so, I sometimes had to take on the task. But I found, to my amazement, that it built my credibility and was an added asset. However, I still determined off-line with my buyer what his positions were so that I could "push back" on the stronger disagreements in the privacy of his office.

No matter what level you're working with, how big or small the business, or the nature of the project you're engaged in, explore whether you can become part of an internal team in a formal or informal sense. In effect, you

Action Items

want to replicate your partnership with the buyer at other levels.

Capitalizing on Past Successes

One of the great paradoxes of consulting is that we tend to get blamed for the disasters (which we often deserve) when projects head south, but we seldom receive full credit when the project proceeds according to plan and dramatically improves the client's condition (which is the all-the-more-frequent occurrence). Both of these conditions are our fault, the first through commission, the second through omission, and both are deadly.

Since we're talking here about solidifying business, it's the second that we're concerned about.

While we have a pragmatic and ethical responsibility to share our success with the people who implemented, supported, and even honestly raised legitimate risks about the work, we also have a business need to alert the buyer and potential buyers about our own contributions. Otherwise, a consultant returns six to nine months after a successful project to inquire about more work and, when using the original success story for credibility, is often told:

- We think we would have arrived at the same point anyway.

- You were a stimulus, but we were heading there, which is why we were so anxious to listen to you.

- Actually, without the financial team it never would have been successful.

- We've since discovered some problems (caused internally, of course) that have downgraded some of our earlier expectations.

- We might have made a more substantial investment (in the consultant's help) than it turns out was actually required.

- We had a great team, and we appreciated your external support.

Ever heard any of those? They occur, quiet naturally, because you've been out of sight and out of mind. In this business, absence makes the heart grow into a fossilized rock with no memory.

The solution is to capitalize on success while it's occurring and as it's concluding. That way, even if there is a hiatus between this project and the next (which shouldn't be happening if you've read Chapter 6), you can readily point to the documentation, discussions, and details of your past "victories" for the buyer.

Here's how.

Establish short-term as well as long-term metrics

Create with the buyer metrics that will indicate success during the project, not solely 18 months later, after the project is completely implemented and, chances are, long after you've departed from it. For example, if your project's objectives include improving the retention of new hires through a redesigned hiring and qualifying process, a long-term measure might be the reduction of turnover at the one-year mark. But you can also have short-term measures: reduction of turnover at the six-month mark; 10-day interviews with new hires that indicate that they feel the hiring experience was positive and informative, and consistent with what they actually found on the job; and 45-day interviews with the new hire's manager to indicate that the skills, behaviors, and attitudes were what was expected after the person has begun independent operations on the job.

Thus, you're able to substantiate the success of your design, even though the ultimate measures might have to await the normal year's assessment. Nevertheless, these metrics can aid substantially in justifying your work in similarly redesigning the performance evaluation system or the compensation system.

Action Items

Visit the buyer regularly

You wouldn't abandon a child, a pet, or even a prized possession. Why on earth would you abandon a buyer after working so hard to build that relationship in the first place?

By visiting the buyer frequently[2] you are able to accomplish two things. First, you can report on successes and reinforce the positive, early developments. While the sales force may not yet have boosted sales, you can report that the call sheets demonstrate that the high-priority clients now account for 85 percent of all sales calls, up from less than 50 percent when you began the project.

Second, you can ask the buyer, "How are we doing?" Buyers will often refrain from seeking you out with bad news. They might also have a hundred priorities that relegate news that's important to you to the bottom of their list. I once learned in one of these 30-minute "updates" that I was ecstatic about the job vacancies disappearing in finance while the buyer was troubled that we weren't making the same progress in the more important R&D area, which he had never before told me was a priority! I was thus able to rapidly shift gears to show early success there as well.

Document progress

While I'm not very big on reports, I do consider it essential to document progress for my interests as well as the buyer's. I do this in two ways.

First, I write notes—usually e-mail, which is easily saved and stored—to anyone pertinent when we have a success. This is a small but vital technique in capitalizing on past and current successes. For example, if the survey work was completed ahead of schedule with a record company participation making for highly valid patterns of information, drop a note to the human resource director, thanking her staff, and citing those particular "victories." If you don't do this, the small stuff goes unnoticed and unnoted. You'll soon have a bulging computer file.

Second, capture everything sent to you that indicates success of any kind. I call this a "rave reviews" file that should be a part of your client file. (There are usually two, one on the computer and one hard copy, unless you're a fanatic about scanning into the computer all of those hard-copy pages.) These communications are important because they constitute an unsolicited critical mass of substantia-

[2]I suggest at least once every two weeks during the initial months of a project, and then at least once a month thereafter, but those are the bare minimums. Weekly meetings for 30 minutes are my favorite, if you're on site anyway.

tion for early successes. Since no one, in all likelihood, is compiling a similar "poor reviews" file, you've got all the momentum in your favor.

> Sales Skills 707: There will occasionally be resisters and threatened people who gather evidence on problems and contradictions about any project. We tend to spend too much time dueling with them. By compiling your own documentation of successes and small victories, you'll have ample validation for your buyer that things are proceeding ahead of plan, and that the inevitable resistance to change has inevitably surfaced.

Create the long-term implementation plan and attendant risks

No matter how successful a project seems to be unfolding, never simply walk away patting yourself on the back. Create a simple but powerful tool for the client for ongoing refinement and protection.

I call this the "long-term implementation plan." Demonstrate, in writing, why you've (collectively) been successful initially and then detail the following:

- Potential problems that can still emerge and that must be prevented or addressed.

- Key internal players who are required to ensure continuing success.

- Specific problems that you've corrected that cannot be allowed to reappear after you're gone.

- The buyer's personal accountabilities for the project's future.

- Further, more dramatic gains that can be accomplished through certain actions.

This delineation of accountabilities enables you, if necessary, to review them months later to point out that any dilution in the project's effectiveness was not caused by overly optimistic expectations when you were present and measuring early results, but rather from a lack of proper care and feeding after you departed the scene. Perhaps they need you back to make things right again?

Action Items

By taking the pains to document successes through early measures, maintain positive feedback with the buyer, and organize the effort for long-term success, you're positioning the buyer to succeed and yourself to return. That's your basic win/win.

Sales Stories

When I was helping an international consulting firm to change its approaches on how it created and submitted proposals, part of the project involved workshop sessions with sales leaders and managers, during which we'd actually review and dissect past and pending proposals.

During one such session I was pointing out the weaknesses of a "take it or leave it" proposal with no options, when one of the managers leapt to his feet, mumbled an excuse, and raced from the room with his cell phone in his hand.

He later told me during lunch that he was sorry for his behavior, but the point I was making had tremendous impact on a two-million-dollar proposal that his office was sending out that day, and he wanted to make sure he reached the London office (five hours ahead of us) to make changes before the office closed and the proposal was mailed.

I asked him to relate that episode to the full group that afternoon. Both the chairman and the president were in attendance. It's the most dramatic example I have of real-time, significant results immediately demonstrated to the buyer. (They eventually closed the deal, for more money than in the original proposal, but it took an additional two months. I was able to show the power of our approach immediately.)

Always Vigilant, Never Complacent

I want to reiterate that there is nothing immoral, illegal, or unethical about seeking out additional business while you are in the midst of delivering current business. This small fact is what totally resolved the ancient bromide, "You can't market while you're delivering. You can't be in two places at the same time, especially if you're a solo practitioner."

That's simply untrue, because you can be involved in two (or more) initiatives at any one time. The computers call it "multitasking." The humans call it "versatility."

The absolute best way to solidify and expand existing business—gather the renewals that are the annuity of any professional sales process—are to be vigilant and aware of your environment. Figure 7-1 demonstrates the sources and the connections that expanded business requires.

Sales Challenge #14

The buyer tells you that you've done such an outstanding job in resolving the teamwork issues in sales that he immediately wants you to leave that group—even though you had planned to work with them for an additional 30 days—and begin working with his own direct reports. You are to submit a proposal quickly and money is no problem.

Besides writing the new proposal and gathering the requisite information for it, do you do anything else?

Meet the challenge.

You might call this vigilance "internal networking." You need both to reach out to other areas and people who might provide additional business, and to position yourself as an approachable resource for those who might not be immediately reachable.

Action Items

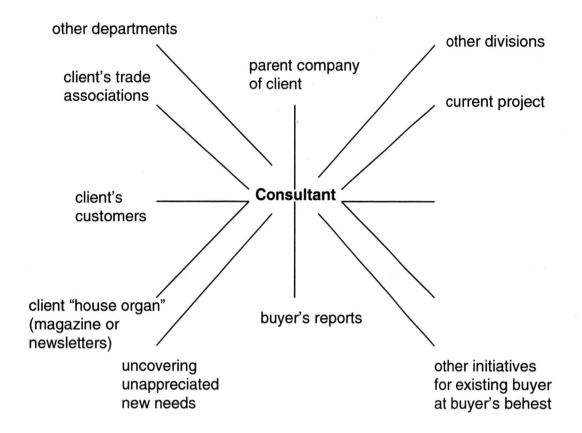

Figure 7-1: The potential for "internal networking"

Sales Skills 709: View your relationships in an account as "internal networking." Just as you network to attract business as a part of normal marketing efforts, do the same thing internally, within existing clients. The process is exactly the same, except you have the advantage of being known and trusted inside the client.

Do you (or your people) have a plan established to seek out and develop the dozen areas around the internal networking map illustrated in Figure 7-1? Think about it: Every month you're working in existing accounts that carry the potential of at least 12 paths to expanded work (and actually many more, since each route on the map can lead to multiple potential). What is your plan for exploit-

ing those areas? In how many existing accounts have you closed business in those areas? In how many have you even inquired about or pursued?

Every day, people providing professional services are leaving money on the table, and nowhere is this worse than in the virtual disregard for repeat and expanded business from existing clients. When this business is pursued, it's often too little, too late—long after the project has ended and the consultant has departed. Picture someone who has managed to land excellent seats for a sold-out play determining that they must go outside at intermission and find two similar tickets all over again in order to watch the second act! Yet, that's what most of us do when we leave the client after the first act or, worse, sometimes after only the first scene.

When the big, overblown remake of *Mutiny on the Bounty* was produced 30 or so years ago, it was so long that it included an intermission, a rarity for a motion picture. As the lights came up after the first part, the crowd stood and began to move toward rest rooms and the concession

Action Items

stand. But four people seated behind us picked up their belongings and departed, saying, "That was disappointing. We don't even know if they got away with it or not." They thought it was over. Is that how you act with clients?

Use my networking map to organize systematic and dedicated approaches toward increasing existing client business *while you're still there to do so*. It's much easier to sell to existing pleased clients, so why leave the building just because the lights have come up and Act I is drawing to a close?

As Yogi Berra observed, "It ain't over till it's over." Don't allow it to end prematurely.

> Sales Skills 710: It is a reasonable expectation that any client can engage you for a multiplicity of projects over several years. These are not events, but rather relationships. The greatest detriment to obtaining frequent and ongoing business is the consultant. The client is actually quite willing.

Self-assessment

How well are you:

- Solidifying your position and relationship with the buyer on an ongoing basis?
- Being perceived as a "part of the client's team"?
- Developing short-term measures and successes?
- Protecting yourself against perceived diminished returns in the future?
- Using a networking map to exploit all potential client business?

Challenge Responses:

#13: You ask the buyer for a few more minutes one-on-one, and explain that you'll need to meet at least once a month for 30 minutes. Further, during this crucial initial aspect of the project, you'll need to keep in touch by e-mail or fax while the buyer travels. This is all key to the

investment's protection and success. Do this in private and immediately.

#14: Tell the buyer that you'd like to work on both groups concurrently to ensure the success of the first one and to use with the second one the lessons learned from the first. If that is impossible logistically or unacceptable to the buyer, then put in writing the steps required and the accountabilities to provide for continued success of the first team, and have the buyer agree to them, documented in a summary letter from you.

Summary of Sales Skills 700

Sales Skills 701: Make no mistake about it: You face a far greater threat from internal client dynamics and opposition than you ever do from external consulting competition. Yet we are much more alert to and prepared for the latter than the former.

Sale Skills 702: After the hard work of reaching a buyer and closing business, to abandon that relationship is like climbing Mount Everest and deciding not to look at the view before heading down again. Abandon the peak at your own peril, because most people don't make the climb a second time.

Sales Skills 703: Team members support each other, establish rapport, suffer common defeats, and rejoice in common victories. A team stands together. If you are a part of such a team, let the momentum sweep you past the rapids and into the deep, blue water.

Sales Skills 704: Not only will you become part of the team by attending ongoing meetings, but you will also quickly learn the often hidden dynamics of power, influence, and persuasion that the key players exert with one another. You may just find that you've missed the true power brokers by looking at title instead of influence.

Sales Skills 705: If you're going to be part of a team, contribute. Don't sit back and watch. The more you actively help the group, the more you'll learn, the more you'll be accepted, and the more you'll be engaged long-term.

Sales Skills 706: Too few consultants go to the buyer regularly and ask, as New York City's Mayor Koch used to ask pedestrians on their way to work, "How am I doing?" They seem to allow the fear of "bad" feedback to destroy their chances of gaining positive and important feedback to validate their contribution.

Sales Skills 707: There will occasionally be resistors and threatened people who gather evidence on problems and

Action Items

contradictions about any project. We tend to spend too much time dueling with them. By compiling your own documentation of successes and small victories, you'll have ample validation for your buyer that things are proceeding ahead of plan, and that the inevitable resistance to change has inevitably surfaced.

Sales Skills 708: If you don't blow your own horn, there is no music. Or, as baseball pitcher and Hall of Fame member Dizzy Dean once said, "If you can do it, it ain't braggin'."

Sales Skills 709: View your relationships in an account as "internal networking." Just as you network to attract business as a part of normal marketing efforts, do the same thing internally, within existing clients. The process is exactly the same, except you have the advantage of being known and trusted inside the client.

Sales Skills 710: It is a reasonable expectation that any client can engage you for a multiplicity of projects over several years. These are not events, but rather relationships. The greatest detriment to obtaining frequent and ongoing business is the consultant. The client is actually quite willing.

Action Items

Chapter 8

Revisiting Former Clients

Hey, remember me?

Many professionals view past clients the same way they view a mausoleum: One should show respect toward them, remain very quiet in the halls, don't spit on the floor, and, above all, don't hang out there. Value the memories, but don't disturb the dead.

I view former clients as off-balance-sheet assets. They comprise high potential value for you and your business *if* the asset is exploited. Empty land in Texas does you no good, and you have to pay taxes on it (you're probably saving client files in hard and/or electronic copy somewhere, taking up space—show me a consultant, for example, who throws away files). But if you authorize drilling on the land as a sensible investment and prudent risk, you just might strike oil.

There are sales professionals reading this book, right now, who own the equivalent of thousands of square acres of vacant land all over the country. They are paying the taxes and performing the rudimentary maintenance—and sometimes even selling off the lots—instead of drilling down to see what's underneath.

One successful, gushing oil well more than pays the bill for all that exploration.

The problem is that the longer the land is left unexplored, the more difficult it is to do anything with it. You get squatters, vermin, interfering neighbors, legal claims, and all kinds of impediments.

How to Maintain Contact

Everyone with whom you've worked is a client. Some are simply current clients, and some are past clients. Every buyer who has retained your services is a buyer, either current or past. Once you have that philosophy, you have an easy mission: to ensure that all buyers (and, therefore, the organizations they represent) are *contemporaries in their relationships with you.*

> Sales Skills 801: You can make all buyers, past and present, *contemporary relationships* by never surrendering the initiative to remain in contact. That is the key preventive action to avoid clients from disappearing and your off-balance-sheet asset from becoming worthless.

The preventive action is never to lose the relationship, and that initiative is incumbent on you to maintain. Staying in touch with your buyer through the project completion and indefinitely into the future creates two salutary situations:

1. Your name is constantly and repeatedly introduced and, sooner or later, the timing will be favorable for consideration in another project.

2. If the buyer changes positions, either within the company or outside of the client organization, you'll learn about it quickly and be able to:

   a) create contact with another buyer within the client

   b) follow the old buyer to the new organization and reestablish contact

After a successful project, one that has shone favorably on client and buyer, maintaining that crucial relationship should be easy—all "downhill." But more than 90 percent of the time, in my unscientific canvassing of people in my mentoring program, the relationship is abandoned by the consultant. That is not the equivalent of leaving money on the table. That is the equivalent of going to the bank, withdrawing your savings, and burning the bills.

Here are the best techniques I know of for maintaining contact with prior buyers and past clients. The good news is that you don't have to implement all of them. But if you use just a couple, you'll be in a much better position than

Action Items

simply saying, "I'd love to work with you again, call me if you need me."

Techniques for maintaining contact:

1. ESTABLISH THE PLAN DURING THE PROJECT WORK.

About three-quarters of the way through your project, if none other is in sight and you've been unable to expand business laterally while you're there, suggest to the buyer that it would be unethical of you to abandon him or her after the final report is completed or implementation step taken. Tell the buyer that you usually establish a mechanism for ongoing dialogue in case you're needed, and as a normal part of the existing project (and fee). *Then provide options:* Would the buyer prefer a monthly phone call? An electronic newsletter, a quarterly meeting, a weekly fax? And so on. By providing this "choice of yeses," you'll greatly raise the probability that the buyer will agree to an alternative that is best suited to personal needs (e.g., a phone call is interactive, but a newsletter is more passive). Implement the choice within a month of the end of the current project.

2. CREATE AN AGENDA OF VALUE.

Don't maintain contact with "How are you doing?" as your most incisive question. In fact, be rather aggressive. Provide value, just as you provided value in the early stages of your relationship. Except now that you know the buyer's style and work demands intimately, you can provide much more focused value. These can take the form of suggestions, Web site referrals, cassettes, book recommendations, experiences from your other clients, new approaches, and so forth. It's vital that the buyer *look forward* to your interactions because they are of use to him, not dread them because they're seen as your personal agenda.

3. ESTABLISH ALTERNATIVE CONTACT POINTS.

If possible, don't restrict yourself to a single vulnerable link. A phone call can be tough with a buyer who travels extensively. E-mail might not work well with a non-technologically inclined buyer. Meetings are problematic if you have to travel a long distance to get there. The best approach is to use a phone call, include the buyer on a monthly newsletter list, send occasional and random articles or position papers, network at trade association meetings, and so on. In other words, don't put all your efforts into one option that can be inadvertently undermined.

> Sales Skills 802: The line between follow-up and "hunting" is not a thin one. If you're constantly out for yourself only and trying to secure additional business, the client will need the ghostbusters. But if you're regularly supplying value and help for the buyer's business, you're engaged in very professional follow-up and the chances are strong that no one will be slimed.

4. BE ABSOLUTELY CONSISTENT AND RELIABLE IN YOUR ROUTINE.

I've been victimized by my own sloth on several occasions when I was too busy or unable to make contact, and allowed six months or more to go by, only to find that the buyer had left or *someone had forgotten how to get in touch with me!* (That has happened to us to our knowledge, so imagine how often it happens to us *without* our knowledge!) If it's a monthly electronic newsletter, don't miss an issue. If it's a quarterly call and the buyer is in Ulan Bator, find out when she will return and make up for lost time. Do not abandon your routine under any circumstances. Remember, the onus is on you to nurture the relationship.

5. INCLUDE RANDOM AND UNPLANNED CONTACT.

Rip out a relevant article from a magazine and pop it into the regular mail. Arrange to have a drink at a trade association meeting you're both attending. Send a card when a child graduates from college, on a 30th anniversary, or for the relevant holidays. Among your routine mechanisms, create spontaneous contact, as well.[1]

6. KEEP CURRENT WITH THE TRADE PRESS AND BUSINESS NEWS.

I had breakfast with a former buyer because I had noticed her promotion in a local business publication, sent my

---

[1]Be careful about holiday gifts, though. Many organizations have clear ethics policies prohibiting acceptance. And those tacky calendars and "Successories" paperweights are usually tossed or relegated to a drawer. Does someone really want to whip out a cheap pen with your name on it at an important meeting? I doubt it . . .

Action Items

congratulations, offered breakfast or lunch, and was immediately accepted. Be vigilant with local sources if your client is in your community, and with trade and professional sources within the client's industry. You can obtain information about a wealth of useful subjects: the buyer, the client, the industry, the competition, the technology, new trends, and so on. What you learn forms an excellent justification for more contact and more value.

Sales Stories

By keeping contact with one particular buyer, I was able to secure work in three different major banks. Another took me from a major pharmaceutical company into a major chemical company. A third took me from health care to food flavorings.

My favorite example is a vice president in an insurance company, who left to become an executive at an industry trade association and "took me along." Our next stop, about two years later, was at a large charitable foundation. Then, sure enough, he became bored and launched his own business, which also necessitated my help. He's since retired, but has asked me to help out with one of the boards he continues to serve on.

I never wish anyone ill, but I don't mind job-hopping at all! Since I'm a process consultant, and I realize my relationship is with the buyer and not the organization, I can be very light on my feet.

"Have consulting skills, will travel."

Plan to implement your "continuing relationship" strategy as soon as you realize that the current project will end without another arising. The best time to do it is while you're still there.

Dealing with New Buyers

What happens when:

- Your buyer is fired?
- Your buyer is transferred?
- Your buyer retires?
- Your buyer goes on long-term disability?
- Your buyer changes jobs voluntarily?
- A reorganization "demotes" or de-emphasizes your buyer?
- For whatever reasons, you simply lose track of the buyer?

It's time to establish a relationship with the new buyer.

Sales Skills 803: While the buyer constitutes your personal relationship, the organization is part of your business relationship, and you can use that to establish contact with new buyers. However, you have to start from scratch with your personal relationship-building. In fact, you might be starting from less than scratch.

New buyers have their own agendas, their own preferences and, often, their own consultants. Nonetheless, you can represent an intelligent and viable value to them if you manage the dynamic correctly.

We've all been subject to the new buyer who doesn't return our calls. In fact, if the previous buyer has left under less-than-ideal circumstances (e.g., fired, joined the competition, blew an assignment, etc.), then that shadow may also engulf you. Additionally, there are often subordinates still in position who didn't exactly relish your interventions, and who now have the opportunity to mortally wound you with their new boss.

The odds aren't exactly stacked in your favor. But the situation is far from hopeless. Let's review the ammunition that you still possess:

Action Items

- You've completed one or more successful projects with documentation against objectives and evidence of results.[2]

- You have other, positive contacts in the organization, perhaps among the subordinates, who will attest to your competence, results, and charm.

- You know the organization very well, and in fact have been paid to be educated about its workings.

- Your "footprint" (written reports, changed procedures, new image, training classes, and so on) may appear quite visibly within the client.

- You are familiar with internal dynamics, culture, and decision-making protocols.

- You know the organization's ongoing strengths and vulnerabilities and, consequently, what still constitutes value and assistance.

> Sales Skills 804: When the old buyer disappears, for whatever reason, start to train the heavy artillery on the new buyer. Use every bit of your knowledge and experience with the organization to create more value for him or her. If you don't blow your own horn, there is no music.

Given these considerable strengths, you can now organize a strategy to contact the new buyer and create the tactics that will be most effective in gaining rapid attention. Everything you do must be around *some value proposition*. If you can't do that amount of homework and preparation, knowing what you know and having been where you've been with that client previously, then you don't deserve another shot.

Here's the difference between mindless attempts at contact without a value proposition, and an intelligent strategy based on that value proposition:

Poor: "My name is Jane Smithers, and I worked with your predecessor. I thought it would make sense for us to meet and review what happened before your arrival."

Strong: "My name is Jane Smithers, and I have a report commissioned by your predecessor on the reasons for poor sales closing rates and what can be done to improve them without capital investment. It was never completely reviewed, and it's important I do this with you personally while the issues are still timely. The debrief is covered under my prior contract."

Poor: "I'm James Scott calling to see if I can set up a meeting or a phone call with Ray Johnston. I was consulting here a year ago, and I thought I could introduce myself should he have similar needs in the future."

Strong: "Please ask Mr. Johnston to call me. I have material, recommendations, and observations from a recent consulting assignment that need to be personally shared and delivered to him. My duty to your organization is not completed until that is done."

Sales Challenge #15

The secretary you have always dealt with tells you that your old buyer has left for another company, and a reorganization has eliminated her position. There is no equivalent manager now.

What do you do immediately?

Meet the challenge.

Poor: "Ray, this is Alan Weiss, and I used to work with Trudy when she was in your position. I'd like to introduce myself and review what we did together. I think I can be of help to you, as well."

Strong: "Mr. Johnston, this is Alan Weiss. I've served as a consultant to your organization, and have assembled a position paper on the chronic problems you've been facing in entering the e-commerce business. I'd like your permission to FedEx™ this to you—it's highly confidential—and then make myself available to discuss the implications and respond to your questions. This is all covered under my prior agreement with your company."

It may sound like you're providing a lot of value and doing a lot of work, and that's because you are. The best way to reach a new buyer is to create a value proposition that is reasonable (a continuation or summation of past project work), pragmatic (no expense at all), emotionally appealing (confidential, addressing a key problem or opportunity), and without obligation (covered by existing agreements).

---

[2]If you don't create that kind of documented trail, then you'd better read my book *The Ultimate Consultant* (Jossey-Bass/Pfeiffer: 2001).

Action Items

> Sales Skills 805: Buyers can readily resist "old" consultants associated with past regimes. But they can't wait to get their hands on "new" value, unexpected help, which might get them off to a running start in their new position. Don't position yourself; position the value to the buyer. It's not about your past, it's about the buyer's future.

On the assumption that the client organization is large enough in potential to you to justify the time and commitment, your best possible strategy is to create *future value* for the new buyer, even if that value rests upon your past work. But it's deadly to base your approach on your old relationships, which mean less than nothing to the new buyer.[3]

It's more essential than ever to present yourself as a potential partner and existing peer, not as a former partner—or worse, salesperson—trying for another sale. Ironically, perhaps, you have to approach the new buyer with the attitude of high value and an offer of help, but not one of desperation and need. In other words, as in most sales opportunities, your ability to present a respected, collegial image—and your willingness to "walk away" from the potential business—are important attributes in creating a new relationship.

Awakening the Dead

There are some clients who are dormant and on the verge of becoming extinct. You haven't been there in five years or more. You've lost contact with the buyer. The place has reorganized. Or moved! They've been acquired, or divested, or been bought out by management. They've gone through bankruptcy and emerged.

In this economy and in these times, such conditions aren't rare. And even with fairly stable client organizations, the sloth of the salesperson may have resulted in a loss of contact, records, and even memory. (Recently, in creating a new corporate brochure for my firm, I revisited every client list from all my years in business. I couldn't identify—couldn't *recognize*—about 10 percent of the list. Hence, my inclusion of this segment in this chapter!)

One solution, of course, is simply to treat these prodigal sons as new business, since your ties are broken and your momentum stopped. And that is always a valid approach. You can apply the first five chapters of this book and ignore the fact that you once worked there and they once paid you, presumably for your value to them.

However, since new business is *always* harder to acquire than repeat business, wouldn't it make more sense to investigate whether there is some way you can turn your prior experience there into at least a lukewarm *rapprochement?* Toward that end, here is a battle plan that might make Dr. Frankenstein proud: a plan to systematically pull together facts, history, expertise, and institutional memory and create new life.

Here's how to awaken the dead.

Battle Plan for Resuscitating and Reviving "Dead" Clients

1. THOROUGHLY STUDY AND REVIEW YOUR OLD FILES.

These days, this should increasingly be a computer exercise, but many of us still have paper files in our offices, garages, and rented storage spaces. This is a good opportunity to finally jettison them (hard and electronic copy), *after* you've withdrawn what's needed for your scheme.

Comb the files for *every* single organization you've done business with, no matter how large or small, with which you have not been in contact in the past two years. Make a note of their names on a sheet of paper, then keep a single file with whatever contact information and past project information you have about them. Don't make judgments, just make piles. (Include *everyone*, even if it's business you wouldn't accept today or a note from when you simply made a paid speech at a management conference.)

2. PERFORM TRIAGE.

Assess your result using three criteria:

a) Know that they are still in business and a going concern.

b) Uncertain of their status.

c) Know that they no longer exist.

Throw out the "c" category files. Put the "b" category aside for now. We'll focus on the "a" past clients.

---

[3]Exception: The old buyer was promoted and is not a senior executive in the same organization. But then you should continue to deal with him, anyway.

Action Items

> Sales Skills 806: There are either clients or nonclients. Of the former, some are active and some are inactive. There is no limbo. Most consultants make virtually no attempt to turn inactive clients into active clients, which is always easier than turning nonclients into clients.

3. PERFORM LOGISTICS INVESTIGATION ON THE CLIENTS.

Determine their current address and whereabouts. Make a call to the switchboard to find out whether your prior contacts are still there and, if so, *what their current positions and contact information are.*

If your past contacts are still there, jump to Step 5. If not, proceed to Step 4.

4. IDENTIFY NEW CONTACTS.

If your past contacts are gone, find out who has replaced them. If there are no direct replacements due to reorganizations and consolidations, then find out who the buyer would be for the kind of value proposition you're offering today.[4] Use the switchboard, annual report, business news, and networking to determine who, for example, serves as vice president of sales, director of the call center, head of retail banking, and so on.

> ## Sales Stories
>
> I'm speaking at a trade association conference in the newspaper industry. After my keynote, an audience member seeks me out and asks if I remember the name of a certain newspaper. I vaguely do, or at least I think I do.
>
> "You should, you worked with us about eight years ago to develop a more aggressive approach in our advertising sales. Remember, it was the first off-site meetings we'd ever had?" Dimly, slowly, the mist begins to clear.
>
> "We've been purchased, and our new parent loves our sales force and its approach. We lost touch with you, then I noticed you were speaking at this conference. Would you like to meet our new corporate owners and discuss doing the same work for their other five operations? They also have some radio outlets that could use help."
>
> "Ah, yes, sure, that's great," I assertively reply.
>
> "Well, at least give me your card. You're the softest selling source of tough sales skills I've ever met!"
>
> I took the work, even though I really didn't deserve it . . .

5. CREATE A "REASSAULT" PLAN.

With either the old contacts still in place or their replacements, use your prior history to create a reason for talking to you. For example, you could be honest and say that you're contacting all clients whose work was more than five years ago so as to make available new learning and new techniques you've developed since then.

You could also send along some articles that appeal to the industry or the buyer. The key is to do some homework and combine your past work for them with some contemporary needs to create at least a "lukewarm" reception.

6. FOLLOW UP AGGRESSIVELY.

You have absolutely nothing to lose here. After your mailing, call and seek a meeting. If that doesn't work, then keep trying. Include the contacts on your mailing lists. Send them your newsletter. Send articles and other references that may be of value. Let them know when you'll be in the neighborhood.

Especially helpful: Send along your testimonials, garnered *since* you worked with them, to illustrate your own continuing growth and credibility in the profession.

---

[4]This isn't the place for the discussion, but your marketing should always revolve around your value proposition, who buys such value, and how to reach that buyer. See my book *Million Dollar Consulting* (McGraw-Hill: 1992, 1998, 2002).

Action Items

7. EXTEND THE ATTEMPT.

Go to your "b" organizations, find out their circumstances, and separate them into your "a" and "c" categories. Then take the new additions to the "a" list and begin at Step 1.

8. DON'T ALLOW THIS TO EVER HAPPEN AGAIN.

Ensure that all more recent (and certainly all new) clients are part of an active campaign to remain in contact and to aggressively seek further business with them. The first half of this chapter—and the entire second half of this book—pertains to that strategy.

Sales Challenge #16

You approach an old client organization, and the new vice president of operations says, "Our policy for the past several years has been to use internal people only, so we haven't hired external help at all. I'm sorry, but we've remained steadfast in that philosophy."

What, if anything, do you do now?

Meet the challenge.

Not every dead client can be brought back to life, even with lightning and bubbling vats of chemicals. That's why I favor the triage system and a step-by-step, methodical approach. Nonetheless, it's criminal at least not to try. Once or twice in our careers, we'll find this amazing dusty warehouse of old clients with which we've lost contact and done nothing. If we're able to get just a few sales from that group at a low cost of acquisition, then why not make the try?

You have such a trove of past clients because you've been good at what you do and you've pleased the vast majority of buyers. Capitalize on that. Unsuccessful salespeople don't have past clients.

Overcoming Poor Experiences

There is a final, unappetizing possibility to explore. In some instances, we've blown it.

Not to worry: Every one of us who is taking risks, innovating, and being at all contrarian will sooner or later fail. Moreover, many of us doing mainstream, intelligent, nonthreatening work will be undone by the forces of darkness (the competition, internal politics, etc.). If you haven't failed in this business, there are only three possible explanations:

1. You've never tried anything daring or exciting.

2. You've failed and just don't realize it.

3. You're lying.

Here are some of the reasons for poor experiences with clients, the preventive action, and the contingent action. In other words, you want to avoid it, but what do you do if you haven't been able to avoid it?

1. POOR-QUALITY WORK.

Situation: Your work has not been up to the quality expectations of the buyer. For example, you missed deadlines, workshops were poorly received by the participants, negotiating skills have not worked, consensus not achieved, and so on.

Preventive: Create clear expectations with the buyer that the nature of your work *and not the results themselves* is what you can guarantee. Ensure that you have the requisite competency to perform the work, and you're not just grabbing money or overstretching (a fa-

Action Items

cilitator does not an organization development consultant make, nor is an insurance salesperson necessarily a financial planner).

Contingent: Provide continued help at no fee until the situation is resolved to the buyer's satisfaction. Return a part or all of the fee. Offer to bring in another resource. Or, just clear out. If you've personally failed because you weren't up to the challenge, it may just be best to clear out.

Sales Stories

I had "guaranteed" the results of my work at a bank in Connecticut. I had thought the vice president to be a lightweight and the staff atmosphere to be highly cynical, but I knew that I could walk on water. Besides, $15,000 for two days of work in the late '80s seemed like a license to print money.

The staff had no intention of implementing my approaches, and the vice president had no intention of changing the reward system, evaluation system, or feedback system to support such change. After about a month of nothing happening, he called to remind me of my "guarantee."

I returned his money, was furious with myself, and have never had that problem again. I guess it was fortunate this happened early in my career for a relatively small amount (at least in retrospect). Loren Eisley once wrote, "Certain coasts are set aside for shipwreck."

Stay away from those coasts, and also make sure that the lifeboats are in working order.

2. INTERNAL OPPOSITION.

Situation: The buyer was enthused and everyone was quick to provide the politically correct lip service, but once under way, the passive aggressive opposition killed the project. Deadlines were missed, promised help was not forthcoming, pilot sites never materialized. People undermined you with the buyer until you were the "black hat."

Preventive: Seek out the informal and formal sponsors and leaders, and co-opt them by providing that their own self-interests will be met. Get the key parties to agree on accountabilities and put them in writing for them and the buyer. Establish a calendar and meetings and confront delay or failure as soon as it happens. Meet with the buyer weekly during new projects. Let the staff know that the spotlight is on them, not you. Always try to be paid at the front end of a project, or shortly thereafter. This creates pressure to continue the project and not fire the consultant.

Contingent: Document what's happened using observed behavior and facts (not supposition and pop psychology) and explain to the buyer that more sponsorship and clout is needed. Suggest that a "clearing of the air" is needed. Stress that the project cannot be successful under these conditions. Draw a line in the sand. It's going to be "them" or you.

Sales Skills 809: Some buyers will attempt to use you as the "club" that they, themselves, are unwilling to bear on their staff or peers. Never take on a project that is a "vendetta" or in which you are the pry bar. We want to create light, but not be the flash point.

3. INTERNAL CONDITIONS CHANGE.

Situation: With the best of intentions, the client company has nonetheless introduced a higher-ranking priority, has suffered an economic reversal, is changing its compensation policy, is moving its headquarters, etc.

Preventive: In your proposal or contract, specify that the buyer and you agree to immediately inform the other of any changes or possibilities that will materially affect the success of the project.[5] Make it clear that

---

[5]See my book *How to Write a Proposal That's Accepted Every Time* (Kennedy Information: 1999).

Action Items

such developments (the buyer learns of a divestiture of the division, you learn that five key salespeople are about to jump ship) will demand that you both reevaluate the future of the project, and make joint adjustments as necessary. Again, it helps tremendously to have been paid in advance or toward the front end of the project.

Contingent: Call a halt and offer to redirect your efforts toward the new priority if you are in any way capable of doing so. Don't allow yourself to become superfluous or irrelevant overnight. Instead, demonstrate that a resource already on board, paid (one hopes), educated about the company, and with the time already allocated, can help with a "running start" on the new initiatives and priorities. Be light on your feet, and don't insist on the continuation of the current project unless you truly believe its contribution becomes more important than ever under the new conditions.

> Sales Skills 810: I've never been in any major project in which conditions didn't change and the unexpected didn't crop up. Agility is far more important than systemization, and nimble can be better than rigid on almost any occasion. Constantly deploy and check your radar for new blips on the screen. They may not be friendly and may not be enemy: They may just be storm clouds so severe that you need to find the eye of the storm.

The more you're able to handle misfortune and poor experiences on the job, the less likely it is that you'll have a break with a client that prohibits all future contact. Take a hard look at your current work and be sure that you're hoping for the best but preparing for the worst.

Self-assessment

How well are you:

- Maintaining contact with all past buyers and significant others?
- Establishing contact with new buyers in existing and recent clients?

- "Mining" past clients for the possibility of revival?
- Bringing new value, new approaches, and new talents to the attention of past buyers?
- Protecting yourself in current engagements against poor experiences?

Challenge responses:

#15: Two things. First, find out where your previous buyer went, and reestablish contact. Second, given your value propositions, find out the new job title of the people who would now most probably buy such value.

#16: Not much you can do. But I would ask this: "What has your experience been within that strategy? How do you compensate for not being able to tap the experiences of other companies and other industries? How have you performed against your direct competition over the past two years?" If the answers are satisfactory for the buyer, move on. But if you've found a few weaknesses, press for a meeting under this premise: "I respect your position, but given your problems, I think we can agree that flexibility is the key and absolute and inflexible positions can be detrimental to your long-term interests."

Summary of Sales Skills 800

Sales Skills 801: You can make all buyers, past and present, *contemporary relationships* by never surrendering the initiative to remain in contact. That is the key preventive action to avoid clients from disappearing and your off-balance-sheet asset from becoming worthless.

Sales Skills 802: The line between follow-up and "hunting" is not a thin one. If you're constantly out for yourself only and trying to secure additional business, the client will need the ghostbusters. But if you're regularly supplying value and help for the buyer's business, you're engaged in very professional follow-up and the chances are strong that no one will be slimed.

Sales Skills 803: While the buyer constitutes your personal relationship, the organization is part of your business relationship, and you can use that to establish contact with new buyers. However, you have to start from scratch with your personal relationship-building. In fact, you might be starting from less than scratch.

Sales Skills 804: When the old buyer disappears, for whatever reason, start to train the heavy artillery on the new

Action Items

buyer. Use every bit of your knowledge and experience with the organization to create more value for him or her. If you don't blow your own horn, there is no music.

Sales Skills 805: Buyers can readily resist "old" consultants associated with past regimes. But they can't wait to get their hands on "new" value, unexpected help, which might get them off to a running start in their new position. Don't position yourself, position the value to the buyer. It's not about your past, it's about the buyer's future.

Sales Skills 806: There are either clients or nonclients. Of the former, some are active and some are inactive. There is no limbo. Most consultants make virtually no attempt to turn inactive clients into active clients, which is always easier than turning nonclients into clients.

Sales Skills 807: With past clients, drop names and events. Tie yourself to successful innovations and initiatives. Use names of people who have been promoted or who left under very favorable circumstances. But don't tie yourself to regimes fallen out of favor or projects that sputtered and crashed. Do your homework before showing up in class.

Sales Skills 808: It's not that you've failed, it's how you intend to recover. It's not that you've been unfairly blamed or treated, it's how you handle it. It's not what happens to you, it's what you do about it.

Sales Skills 809: Some buyers will attempt to use you as the "club" that they, themselves, are unwilling to bear on their staff or peers. Never take on a project that is a "vendetta" or in which you are the pry bar. We want to create light, but not be the flash point.

Sales Skills 810: I've never been in any major project in which conditions didn't change and the unexpected didn't crop up. Agility is far more important than systemization, and nimble can be better than rigid on almost any occasion. Constantly deploy and check your radar for new blips on the screen. They may not be friendly and may not be enemy: They may just be storm clouds so severe that you need to find the eye of the storm.

Action Items

Chapter 9

The Gold Standard: Retainer Business

When it's just so nice to have you around

I've found that retainer business is the ultimate client relationship, because, in effect, a buyer has said that it would be nice to have you around just to have access to your smarts. And, the buyer is willing to pay for that.

Most retainer business is in combination with other clients' project business and the more routine types of engagements. But there is no magic formula that I know of to represent appropriate amounts of retainer income. I can visualize an all-retainer practice. Any of us can certainly handle multiple retainers, although there are important techniques that will enable that strategy, and we'll discuss them below.

In my experience, it's rare to begin on retainer for a new client. The more normal route is to have completed several projects for an existing buyer who then sees the benefit of simply keeping you accessible rather than periodically engaging you and being subject to availability problems, new contracts each time, reeducation about changes, and so forth.

Consequently, the royal road to retainer business is marked by the abilities we discussed earlier in this book: securing repeat business, attracting new buyers within existing business, and remaining in touch with valuable support with every single past buyer. That being the case, we did not discuss retainers in the first half of the book as a new business acquisition strategy, since they are much easier and more common as an aspect of repeat business and business expansion. (However, the strategy and tactics below can be applied just as readily to a new client and new buyer.)

Converting to "Access to Your Smarts"

Occasionally, a client will suggest that you go on retainer, but it's far more common for the consultant to suggest the transition. Since we've noted earlier that there are no new objections, we need to be prepared to provide a rationale for this arrangement. I've found that it includes the following:

- There is no restriction on the types of issues with which you assist.

- Your education is ongoing, and you don't have to "catch up" with each new issue.

- You have better context and frame of reference.

- The buyer has virtually unlimited access to you.[1]

- There is no need to create new proposals, to get new approval from the legal department, and to access more budget money during the retainer period.

- The client receives priority treatment and time.

> Sales Skills 901: The retainer arrangement is actually sometimes the solution to a buyer's problem about how to use you more but minimize the resistance and/or bureaucracy in his own organization. Retainers must always be "win/win."

Converting to a retainer arrangement also implies that you and the buyer are quite clear on the differences in structure between it and your former project work. Retainers aren't chaos and aren't anarchy. They are simply a different form of a structured relationship. Here are some comparisons:

Project Work	Retainer Work
• Oriented around specific objectives	• Oriented around your talents
• Specific metrics, usually	• Subjective measures
• Value delivered by project results	• Value delivered by general assistance

---

[1]This isn't as tough as it sounds. We'll discuss it in detail below.

Action Items

Project Work	Retainer Work
• Entails implementation	• Entails only advice
• Organizational impact	• Buyer impact
• Front stage	• Behind the scenes
• Organized by project scope	• Organized by time duration
• Unlikely to renew per se	• Likely to renew per se
• Wide diversity of fees	• Less variance in fees
• Varied from client to client	• Consistent from client to client
• Focus on process and content	• Focus almost exclusively on process
• Can involve subcontracting	• Never involves subcontracting
• Proposal required	• Letter of agreement may suffice
• Many client personnel involved	• Very few client personnel involved
• Tendency to publicize results	• May seek to keep results confidential
• Organization skills are key	• Interpersonal skills are key
• Most consultants engage in	• Few consultants engage in

While some of these traits may "cross the line" on occasion, the two columns taken in whole are quite accurate. Retainers are a different animal, and they require different skills and even different relationships.

The timing key in attempting to convert to retainers is in being sensitive to several issues that may develop in the client environment.

The buyer tends to expand project scope regularly

If, with the best of intentions, the buyer is constantly trying to involve you in other issues, especially those not even peripherally associated with your current project, then the buyer has shown a respect for your expertise, a need for your help, and a willingness to ask for it. You can suggest an arrangement, therefore, more in line with the buyer's own self-interests.

Several different buyers are engaging you concurrently for advice

Only you may realize the extent to which you're being utilized by buyers who may not normally talk to each other. In such an event, you may want to broach the subject of a more effective way to work together that won't create internal priority conflicts in terms of your help.

> Sales Skills 902: It's always possible to suggest a conversion to a retainer arrangement. The worst the client can say is "no." The key is to present the conversion as particularly timely, economical, and effective. You are probably the only person in a position to possess all the facts to make this case.

The buyer has tended to use you as a personal counselor, not as an interventionist

If your project role has really worked out to be that of personal advisor and coach, then your best interests are to work toward a retainer relationship because project objectives, no matter how carefully created originally, may not be met by your increasingly "backstage" role. All projects change and evolve, and this evolution is not at all uncommon.

You find that the issues are generally the buyer's issues, not organizational

If the reason for poor teamwork is the buyer's poor leadership, and lack of expansion is due to the buyer's lack of a decent decision-making model, and the poor retention is the result of the buyer's poor choices for key positions, then the solutions are not systemic but rather individual. In fact, the issues you've been asked to address are merely the symptoms of the root cause of the problems.

The buyer "creates" projects in order to keep you around

We've all found ourselves the beneficiaries of "light-weight" projects that a buyer has created as an excuse to keep us handy and "on the books." Instead of merely play-

Action Items

ing along with the subterfuge, suggest a more honest relationship in the retainer arrangement.

When you see any of the above situations developing, the time is ripe to convert the account to retainer business. But it's important to be very clear about that line of demarcation.

Sales Stories

While working on retainer to a *Fortune* 50 high-tech firm, my buyer began "offering me around." Before I knew what was happening, and without prior discussions, she would say to a colleague on a conference call, "Well, Alan is on retainer so why don't you have him come to Dallas and give you some feedback on your strategy session?"

The offer, of course—free help with no strings—was too appealing to resist!

I had to explain the rules again, which was helpful to my buyer and a good reminder for me not to take things for granted. She assumed that I was always available and, if not helping her, should be able to help someone else. I had to explain that I was a consultant on retainer, not a subordinate, and had other clients (and a life!). She was simply trying to get the best deal for her and her organization, which I could completely understand.

Retainers are based on relationships as much as is project work, and maybe more so. You have to be comfortable to step in and redefine the rules and the playing field from time to time. In terms of art and science, retainers lean toward the former.

Sales Skills 903: Retainer work is subject to "midcourse" alteration more than is project work. Expect it, and prepare your buyer for it. It is inadvertently easy for a client to abuse a retainer relationship, *as it is for a consultant to pay insufficient attention to it*. By open communications and through trust, you can avoid both pitfalls.

Free-Form Business vs. Projects

That line of demarcation must be clear in your mind, first and foremost. Your traditional business has been project business; most of your business will be project business; and your daily frame of reference is project business. Hence, you'll need to create clear parameters for yourself in making any transition to retainer business.

1. TIMING AND DURATION

Project work lasts until the objectives have been met. There may be an estimate of that timing, but the key is to meet the objectives. Retainer work is specifically for a defined duration. Project work is baseball—you play until you win (or lose), even into extra innings. Retainer work is hockey—you play until the clock runs out.

Retainer work should be for a minimum of 90 days. Less than that amount of time simply does not provide the necessary duration to achieve very much (in some instances of executive coaching there might be an exception). Retainers for 6, 9, and 12 months are all common. It's often difficult to establish a retainer that transcends a client's fiscal year, but I've seen it happen.

2. PAYMENT TERMS

While I always advocate getting paid in advance, a great deal of project work for most consultants involves a deposit and periodic payments thereafter (sometimes even the noxious "payment on completion"). In retainer work, it's vital to be paid at the beginning of your time period.

In other words, a quarterly retainer should be paid on the first day of that quarter; a semiannual retainer on the first day of those six months, and so on. This is for two rea-

Action Items

sons: First, you want to be free to give unfettered advice, not having to worry about the next month's retainer check if you have to tell the buyer what an oaf she's being. Second, in hard times and sudden change, retainers are frightfully easy to cancel, since they're not attached to a high-priority project. You have to shield yourself from that possibility.

3. CLIENT ACCESS

In project work you generally require access to as many key people as possible, and want to ensure that you're available to anyone who influences the outcome of the project (which is why a project fee rather than an hourly fee is in the best interests of the client). However, in retainer work, you require highly restricted access as part of the arrangement.

You can't very well be on retainer to the buyer and her 12 direct reports, or you'll never be able to eat or sleep. The retainer must be with a single person having access, although you both may agree to admit other people on a limited basis if conditions warrant. Being retained by a team, unless the interactions are highly restricted (e.g., to team meetings only), can become burdensome and unprofitable.

4. IMPLEMENTATION VS. ADVICE

Your mission on retainer is to offer advice; to serve as a counselor and confidante; and to be a sounding board. In project work, of course, your mission is often to assist with implementation, namely: interview employees, visit client sites, design a compensation system, run customer focus groups, facilitate strategic retreats.

As a professional on retainer, your job is to provide counsel on a wide variety of issues but to assist in implementing virtually none of them. In fact, if you find yourself "on retainer" to implement three or four projects, you'll find yourself in a poorly structured engagement. You should have proposed separate project engagements, each with their own fee. Instead, the buyer—wittingly or unwittingly—has pulled a fast one.

> Sales Skills 904: Projects have defined goals and metrics, and end when those measures indicate the goals are accomplished. Retainers have defined time frames and limited access. They end when the calendar indicates they've expired.

5. APPEARANCES AND LOGISTICS

Virtually all projects require that you show up at given intervals. I acknowledge that there are remotely completed projects, and global communications and high technology permit fewer on-site visits than ever before. Nonetheless, there are project requirements that will usually dictate personal interactions, observations, workshops, and so on.

In retainer work, you may also meet with your buyer regularly. Some retainers may call for scheduled meetings, and some might require access only when needed. However, retainers *tend* to rely on e-mail and telephone much more than does project work. They also place a premium on nontraditional timing. Your retainer client may need to talk on Sunday evening before important Monday morning executive committee meetings. Or the buyer might need a relatively quiet Saturday, away from the weekday demands of the office or his travel schedule. Be prepared for more unconventional types, timing, and frequency of communications in retainer work. This is what increases their value.

Sales Challenge #17

Your buyer says that a retainer makes sense, but there's no precedent in the company and the legal department demands that every outside vendor of any kind be justified in terms of specific organizational results, so that a return on investment calculation can be determined.

Do you simply continue with your project work, or is there another choice?

Meet the challenge.

---

6. PERSONAL ACCOUNTABILITY AND LACK OF LEVERAGE

The retainer is based on your personal ability to help the buyer interactively, much more so than is any project. Consequently, some traditional sources of leverage, such as subcontracting, utilizing the client's own resources, and resorting to changes in timing are not options in retainer work.

While you can take on multiple retainer clients without problems, one of the constraining factors is the need for your personal involvement and irreplaceable help. Your talent is what has been purchased, and there is no substitute for it. Retainer clients are lucrative and generally long-lived, which is good news. The bad news is that your personal involvement is the delivery mechanism. You'll have to be sure that supply can more than meet demand.

Action Items

7. RENEWAL BUSINESS IS MORE LIKELY TO OCCUR AND BE MORE PROFITABLE WHEN IT DOES OCCUR

In all selfishness, it is easier to renew a retainer than it is to segue one successful project into another. Since the second half of this book is about repeat business, retainers can be a key and lucrative part of such a strategy.

Rather than limit your scope, as you would in project work, you should seek to *enlarge* your scope in retainer work. Provide the buyer with assistance in tangential areas; bring up your own ideas about new issues to examine; and suggest your willingness to be involved in additional challenges. The more valuable you make yourself *and the less it is connected with a single issue that may disappear or be successfully resolved,* the more likely your retainer will be renewed (and possibly enlarged). I've seen many buyers "automatically" include the consultant's renewal as a core piece of the following year's budget, rather than as a "luxury" that had to be justified against other priorities.

> Sales Skills 905: The key to a project is to be specifically effective in a narrow scope. The key to a retainer is to be generally effective in a wide scope. Neither is mutually exclusive, but these are two separate competencies.

Setting Appropriate Expectations: The Five Ground Rules

Buyers must be reeducated about retainers, no matter how smooth the relationship has been to date. Establishing the correct expectations means the difference between a healthy profit margin and a loss, and between an even better relationship and a rupture. Other than that, it's not important.

If you do nothing, the tendency of the buyer will be to assume that he or she now has your attention full time for as many projects as possible. It's like one of those "all you can eat" buffets that are so popular with already overweight Americans.

Here are the ground rules for this particular relationship. There's nothing wrong with confirming them in your letter of agreement.

Sales Stories

When AT&T was having some of its worst strategy problems under then-CEO Bob Allen, the company had a stated policy of restricting consultants. Some questioned whether that was wise in view of the help that was obviously required.

When Allen was forced into retirement, his replacement found, to nearly everyone's astonishment, that there were consulting retainers, contracts, and agreements in effect that totaled over one billion dollars annually around the company.

That's the degree to which consulting help can become a routine and "automatic" aspect of any organization's budgeting process. While AT&T might not have been using consultants well, my point is that there is an inertia and momentum toward continued use in most large entities.

1. TIMING

There is a finite time involved, which is probably a quarter, a half year, a year, or some total of months. The retainer begins and ends on fixed dates.

Question: Will you allow the buyer to call a "freeze" and stop the clock during periods of vacation, turmoil, business travel, and so on? If so, will it be haphazard or for a month at a time? Will they be unlimited or will only one be allowed? What about the consultant? Can you call a freeze if you see a reason? It's vital to establish these parameters before beginning.

Hint: Don't allow freezes for less than two weeks, and don't allow "thaws"—if you're on a break, then don't allow the client to remain in contact or you've created "scope creep" in a retainer relationship.

Action Items

2. ACCESS

In retainer business, it's usually incumbent on the client to call you for help as needed, which is the "trigger" for your work and direction.

Question: Who will have access and under what conditions? Is the buyer the "trigger," or is it someone he or she designates? Is it more than one person? Can the buyer's staff call you under certain specific conditions (e.g., a key meeting with a customer that requires preparation)?

Hint: Keep access to an absolute minimum or you'll be driven crazy (and to the poor house). Ideally, it should be the buyer, but it might be his designate if the buyer is acting to help a key subordinate. Never allow it to be more than two people (for example, in small businesses there are often two partners who are the owners).

> Sales Skills 906: Establish the rules of the road early, or you'll soon be having disagreements over the best route to the destination. You might naturally choose the fastest alternative, while the buyer might prefer the scenic tour. You have to agree on the criteria.

3. CONTACT

The client is expecting personalized help and priority attention, and will need to be in touch with you at unscheduled times.

Question: How does the client expect, and prefer, to interact? Is the buyer in the same time zone? Does the buyer travel extensively and, if so, domestically or internationally? Does the client travel with access to her e-mail? You must establish not only the scheduled mechanism for communicating (e.g., monthly meetings, weekly phone calls, daily e-mail, and so forth), but also the means for unscheduled needs. Can the client call you "after hours" and at home? Are you on call 24 hours, seven days a week, or only during business hours? If the latter, the client's business hours or your own?

Hint: Maximize off-site contact flexibility and minimize on-site requirements. Most retainer advice can be accomplished by phone, fax, and e-mail. Sometimes you're needed in person to attend a meeting or observe your client, but that's much less common. Hence, offer almost unlimited access so long as it's not abused (e.g., home phone and off-hours are fine, but never before 8 A.M. or af-

ter 8 P.M. your time). Also, *never, ever* offer pager access or keep your cell phone on. Nothing is that urgent, and you're not a heart surgeon. Simply check your voice mail frequently. It does no good for your client or for you to answer a call in a movie lobby or while driving. Be accessible, but not trampled.

4. SCOPE

Your buyer will have a plethora of needs and will, understandably, seek the best help and counsel available, which usually will include you.

Question: On how many issues and to what degree can the client actually expect your help? Are you a sounding board for general issues or an expert on specific areas? Will you help implement and monitor, or simply conceptualize and formulate? This may be the single most crucial area in making sure that the retainer is honorably observed.

Hint: I advise strongly that your retainer responsibility begin and end with advising your client. Once you proceed to implementation, you are engaged in overseeing and executing a project, and that, to me, is no longer retainer work. Make it clear that you are the "backstage" advisor and not the front-stage implementer. Otherwise, the client is piling up more and more plates at the "all you can eat" consulting buffet.

> Sales Skills 907: The line between retainer work and project work is clear and should be drawn in the sand. Once you're asked to proceed beyond advice and actually oversee implementation (e.g., project planning, monitoring, midcourse correction, and so on), you've left the retainer farm and headed for the big city. The big city is much more expensive.

5. PAYMENT

Although you may try to be paid at the front end of project work, you often must settle for a deposit and payments along the way. That is actually rather unhealthy in retainer work.

Question: Will you be paid for the retainer period in advance, or at some other interval? What about extending

Action Items

the retainer? Who decides that, when is it decided, and how is it paid for? This is particularly important for relatively short-lived retainers, but applies to all of them. Should you give incentives to continue?

Hint: Always try to receive full payment for the period in advance (e.g., for a quarterly retainer, the entire amount at the beginning of each quarter). This is important so as not to compromise your ability to honestly provide feedback to the person who is most likely also paying your bill. Also, try to achieve agreement on whether to continue well before the period is up. In a quarterly arrangement, you should discuss this and reach agreement by the second week in the third month of the quarter, if not before. Otherwise, how can you allocate your time and energies effectively, especially if you're dealing with more than one retainer relationship? You can create an "automatic renewal clause" for shorter retainers, meaning they automatically renew unless either party notifies the other at least 30 days in advance of the expiration date of that period. *All retainers should be noncancellable for the periods involved, no exceptions.* If you are paid in advance, this becomes happily academic.

If you do nothing else but cover these five ground rules in your letter of agreement, you'll have gone a long way toward setting the appropriate expectations and safeguarding an important relationship. But it's up to you to take this initiative prior to beginning the retainer relationship.

Sales Stories

I was involved in a retainer with a senior vice president of operations who, literally, traveled the globe. He was on the road about 80 percent of the time, from South Africa to China to Luxembourg. The CEO was the buyer, but the vice president was my client.

We had met once, at his office in California. After that, for six months, we communicated almost exclusively by e-mail. We had one phone conversation while he was in Canada, and another from his office between trips. But other than that, we used e-mail three or four times a week.

The CEO had been somewhat skeptical, but after six months the vice president told him that it was the most successful consulting help he had ever received. It was great for me, since I never had to get on an airplane or even leave my office.

Technology is wonderful for this kind of work, and e-mail easily "shifts" time zones so that they become irrelevant. Technology hasn't changed consulting, contrary to what many "experts" believe, but it can be a tremendous augmentation for our work.

This was a $60,000 project with zero expense and no overhead whatsoever. And it generated a superb testimonial and several referrals. What occurred to me, of course, was how many of those I could maintain concurrently! Hence, my international mentoring program was born and, after six years, has had nearly 200 participants.

Sales Skills 908: There is nothing immoral or unethical or illegal about minimizing physical time present in retainer work. The only question is: Am I living up to my obligations and the expectations of the buyer? Technology and retainer work were made for each other.

Action Items

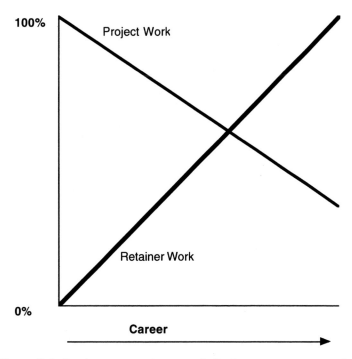

Figure 9-1: Project vs. retainer work during career progression

Balancing Retainers and Other Business

In the trajectory of your career, retainer work should increase and project work decrease as:

- You establish a brand and repute

- You create more and better relationships with key buyers

- You become more experienced and offer more diverse help

- You wish to travel less and derive income from "remote" sources

As you can see in Figure 9-1, at a point about two-thirds of the way through your career you should be transitioning so that retainer work begins to outpace project work and, ultimately perhaps, becomes about 60 percent to 70 percent of your total revenue from these two sources. At the beginning of your career, project work will probably comprise 100 percent of revenues, but that can change as quickly as you gain the attributes noted in the points outlined above.

> Sales Skills 909: The successful professional should have a strategy to create more and more retainer assignments, and to orient marketing initiatives, collateral materials, and, most important, buyer conversations in that direction.

Project work will always play a role, and will be a source for retainer work, since the latter is most easily accomplished through the conversion of existing buyers. But project work needn't continue to be the lion's share of your client base.[2] In fact, if your plans are to write books, retire early, travel more for leisure, spend more time with children and grandchildren, volunteer, pursue hobbies, and/or just plain make changes to keep yourself vital and interested, then you will be *required* to change your business model from the time-consuming project work that generated most of the business to begin with!

[2]"Lion's share" originally meant the entire share, not the predominant part, since the lion kept everything. I use it here with either meaning!

Action Items

You can even balance project and retainer work within a single client, providing a focus on one for buyer "A" and the services of the other for buyer "B." I've even managed to perform both roles for a single buyer, serving on retainer for general issues but also working on individual projects under separate contracts and payment terms. That is a balancing act, to be sure, but it can be done, and there is nothing inherently contradictory about it so long as you both keep clear as to which accountabilities pertain to which endeavors.

Sales Challenge #18

Your buyer loves the retainer arrangement, and wants to transfer and enlarge it to his staff, which is having trouble with teamwork and collaboration. The buyer says to come up with whatever arrangement makes sense, but the six direct reports could use the same kind of personal attention that she's been getting from you.

What's your next move?

Meet the challenge.

I've often reflected that my ideal client is someone who pays me $5 million for an hour of work during the year. (My wife says that if I can work for an hour, then I can work for two hours.) The point, of course, is that value is in the eyes of the beholder.

Selfishly, retainer work appears to be an "easy" way to make money. But pragmatically and realistically, it's an opportunity to assist your buyer in an intimate, flexible, and "real-time" arrangement. There are three keys that determine the "good deal" or the value proposition for the both of you:

1. Does the client receive the practical help on a timely basis that meets the expectations established?
2. Are you paid to reflect that value being delivered?
3. Is the arrangement *less* time consuming and *less* physically demanding than your project work?

Many consultants successfully create retainers only to simultaneously create burdensome, onerous, and exhausting relationships that find them no better than hired hands, constantly on call, and often on site. By following the guidelines in this chapter, I hope you'll realize that retainer relationships are win/win dynamics that can generate substantial profits with less demanding work. At a certain time in your career, they have the potential to serve as huge contributions to expansion business.

The only question is, do you want it?

> Sales Skills 910: You will seldom receive retainers if you don't ask for them. You will seldom be able to ask for one without a strong, preexisting relationship. That is still another reason why effective selling is a relationship business.

Self-assessment

How well are you:

- Asking for retainer arrangements?
- Establishing mutually beneficial guidelines for retainer relationships?
- Increasing your retainer business as a percentage of revenues?
- Balancing project and retainer work?
- Minimizing your travel and the onerous parts of your delivery?

Challenge responses:

#17: Work with the buyer to create a battle plan that demonstrates to the legal eagles that the scope and variety or work you'll be covering together would greatly exceed what the company could afford on an individual project basis. The fact that you're advising and not implementing is not something that need be expressed to the lawyers. It's the value of the advice across a wide spectrum of issues that will make the ROI significant.

#18: Whoa, this is project work, intended to create a better working team among direct reports. Treat it as such. DO NOT attempt a retainer with an additional six individuals, since they need a team approach, not individualized ones, and you will be driven crazy if you try.

Summary of Sales Skills 900

Sales Skills 901: The retainer arrangement is actually sometimes the solution to a buyer's problem about how to use you more but minimize the resistance and/or bureaucracy in his own organization. Retainers must always be "win/win."

Action Items

Sales Skills 902: It's always possible to suggest a conversion to a retainer arrangement. The worst the client can say is "no." The key is to present the conversion as particularly timely, economical, and effective. You are probably the only person in a position to possess all the facts to make this case.

Sales Skills 903: Retainer work is subject to "midcourse" alteration more than is project work. Expect it, and prepare your buyer for it. It is inadvertently easy for a client to abuse a retainer relationship, *as it is for a consultant to pay insufficient attention to it.* By open communications and through trust, you can avoid both pitfalls.

Sales Skills 904: Projects have defined goals and metrics, and end when those measures indicate the goals are accomplished. Retainers have defined time frames and limited access. They end when the calendar indicates they've expired.

Sales Skills 905: The key to a project is to be specifically effective in a narrow scope. The key to a retainer is to be generally effective in a wide scope. Neither is mutually exclusive, but these are two separate competencies.

Sales Skills 906: Establish the rules of the road early, or you'll soon be having disagreements over the best route to the destination. You might naturally choose the fastest alternative, while the buyer might prefer the scenic tour. You have to agree on the criteria.

Sales Skills 907: The line between retainer work and project work is clear and should be drawn in the sand. Once you're asked to proceed beyond advice and actually oversee implementation (e.g., project planning, monitoring, midcourse correction, and so on), you've left the retainer farm and headed for the big city. The big city is much more expensive.

Sales Skills 908: There is nothing immoral or unethical or illegal about minimizing physical time present in retainer work. The only question is: Am I living up to my obligations and the expectations of the buyer? Technology and retainer work were made for each other.

Sales Skills 909: The successful professional should have a strategy to create more and more retainer assignments, and to orient marketing initiatives, collateral materials, and, most important, buyer conversations in that direction.

Sales Skills 910: You will seldom receive retainers if you don't ask for them. You will seldom be able to ask for one without a strong, preexisting relationship. That is still another reason why effective selling is a relationship business.

Action Items

Chapter 10

Postgraduate Course: Referral Business

I'm not leaving this town until I get three names . . .

I'm concluding this book with the most valuable and ignored source of business acquisition that I know of: referral business. Over the past several years, how many people have you referred to your attorney, dentist, physician, landscaper, architect, insurance agent, car dealership, plumber, or electrician? If you're like most of us, you see such referrals as "win/win/win," creating goodwill for all three parties.

Yet how many clients have your professional acquaintances, clients, and vendors provided to you?

Most of us are not receiving the number of referrals we deserve, *not* because people don't like our work or are too busy to remember us, but because *we don't ask for them.* Every day in my mentoring program I deal with consultants, trainers, speakers, and entrepreneurs who say, "I just don't feel comfortable asking for help like that."

My advice? Get over it.

As you progress in the sales profession, you should be building an "annuity" of names, sources, and references that provides an ever-increasing stream of highly qualified leads for your pipeline. The effect is clearly cumulative, and if you start early in the game you derive the benefit relatively early. If you wait too long, you may never realize the benefits.

Let's begin with the easiest, most controllable, and most effective technique: Asking for prospect.

Referrals à la Mapes

When I began my career at the age of 22 at Prudential Insurance, I found that the company assigned an agent to all new employees to sell us a small policy. This was both to support the cause, and also to provide some leads and revenue to the agents.

I still remember my agent's name in 1968: Hal Mapes. Hal sold to my wife and me a tiny policy, because we rented, had no children, and, most important, had no money. But Hal would visit twice a year, like clockwork, to see if any-

thing had changed in our family situation, health, income, and so on. And he'd *never* leave without asking, "Alan, can you give me three names of people who might need insurance?"

I was uncomfortable with supplying names to Hal, and on the third visit I said, "Hal, I just can't think of anyone." He replied, "That's okay, take your time," and asked my wife for another cup of coffee! I realized Hal wasn't leaving without the names, and came up with them quickly enough. In future visits, I had the names ready a week before Hal's appointment.

One day I sat down and worked the numbers: If Hal had 100 clients he was visiting twice a year (200 visits) and received three names each time (600 names) and closed just 10 percent of those leads (60 sales) at an average commission of $3,000, that equaled a new business commission alone of $180,000 in the late '60s! Add to that his annuity commissions from prior sales, and the fact that each year he obviously had more customers, and Hal was making a very handsome income.

> Postgraduate Work #1: Ask every current client for referral business at least once a quarter. Period. If you're not doing that, then you're working very hard to go around the block in order to get next door.

The reason we don't ask current clients for referrals is that we're embarrassed to do so, pure and simple. We seem to believe that we're asking for a handout or a free loan. That philosophy must change. Here are the reasons that referrals make sense for everyone concerned:

1. The client will look good by providing someone they know and respect with high-quality help—you.

2. The client will feel good in doing you a favor that can reasonable be expected to be considered if and when

Action Items

the client needs a favor. (A client asked me recently for a contact in a firm that was a mutual customer, but one she was having trouble penetrating further.)

3. The third party will benefit and be improved.

4. Your own marketing and selling will be considerably eased and improved, enabling you to spend more quality time on clients and more of the margin on your lifestyle requirements.

I've actually asked clients why they haven't provided unsolicited referrals for professional service providers (in other words: Why did Hal always have to *ask?*). Here are the reasons—read them and weep:

- They believed that the individual would resent their name being given to someone without permission.

- They felt that it would be construed as an attempt at a favor or quid pro quo.

- They were uncertain about the professional's capabilities beyond their own immediate experience.

- They didn't want to share the wealth.

- They thought it "wasn't done" in our profession.

> Postgraduate Work #2: Refer potential business to your clients where possible, and make that act known (whether it results in business or not). Then you will have "greased the reciprocal skids."

Everyone reading this book right now should start jotting down on the opposite page the people who will be asked for referral in the next week. My guess is that you can generate a list of at least a dozen people, *better than two a day.* If you have a staff, start them immediately on gathering phone numbers and e-mail addresses. If not, then look up two people a day yourself.

Here are the sources:

- Current clients
    - buyers
    - significant implementers
    - other key people you've met

- Past clients
    - buyers
    - significant implementers
    - other key people you've met

- Social community
    - colleagues on committees, charities, fund-raisers
    - friends: sports, children's events, civic and service clubs
    - social clubs and memberships

- Professional community
    - colleagues in other specialties (noncompete)
    - doctors, attorneys, accountants, other professionals
    - trade associations, professional groups

- Acquaintances and historical
    - alumni associations
    - periodic contacts (e.g., vacations, distant family)
    - former work colleagues from past employment

Add to my list as you see fit, but there is no way that there are fewer than 50 to 100 people you can immediately target without thinking hard. Drop them a note, send an e-mail, make a telephone call. Enclose your brochure, a press kit, a single publicity sheet, one of your articles, or your business card. Remind them of what you do, give them an example of whom you've helped, *but do not ask them to keep you in mind!*

Ask them to give you three names.

Even if you're not as insistent as Hal Mapes, if half of 50 people give you three names, you'll have 75 leads you didn't have before. If you close just 10 percent of the leads, you have seven pieces of new business with virtually zero marketing expense and highly efficient use of your time. (And if your lead generation exceeds that number and your closing success is superior, the sky is the limit.)

Don't forget: From every one of those new sales, ask them for three names.

A note to those of you new to the business, and to those who are such veterans that you may have forgotten: One of the primary reasons to carefully collect and store names is to be able to access people periodically for purposes such as this. With modern software, there is no reason in the world not to create databases that can be segmented

Action Items

into the categories I've listed above, or any others that make sense to you.

Have you filled up the "notes" page with potential referral sources yet? If not, do so now before moving on.

> Postgraduate Work #3: If you find that a pleasant and cordial meeting will not result in business for quite sound reasons, but the relationship is good, try this: "I'm sorry we won't be able to work together, but I'm confident we understand each other's situation. Before I leave, could you recommend to me three or four people who may be able to benefit from my services, now knowing what you know about me?" There is nothing to lose, and you'll usually walk out of an "unsuccessful" sales call with three new leads!

Testimonials

Testimonials are different from referrals. These are "passive" documents that confirm and validate how good we are, to be used at our discretion with prospects. Once again, we value them when they are received without solicitation, but we rarely assertively seek them.

Another big mistake.

I maintain an entire book of testimonials, going back 10 years and extending right up to the current year. I have them printed 20 at a time at the local print shop, so that I can keep adding to it without a large inventory to dispose of. The book contains embarrassing praise on the letterhead of Merck, Hewlett-Packard, Chase, British Standards Institute, American Institute of Architects, American Press Institute, Calgon, and scores of others.

When a prospect receives this booklet with my press kit, guess how many of those testimonial providers are requested as references?

None.

That's because the prospect knows I haven't made all that up and such an overpowering display of consulting prowess is sufficient for credibility and credentials. So let's get on with business.

Sales Stories

The senior vice president at Revlon had promised me a testimonial letter after a successful engagement, yet it never arrived. Two follow-up calls generated apologies and promises, but still it didn't appear.

Finally, I swiped a piece of Revlon stationery and wrote a testimonial that would have embarrassed Donald Trump. I sent it to my buyer with a postage-paid return envelope and this note: "Dear Frank, if you don't provide me with the testimonial you promised in the next week, I'll forge your name on this one and simply use it. Regards, Alan."

Three days later, I had my official testimonial.

The time to request a testimonial *is at the start of the project.* Don't wait until completion, and never delay until you're no longer present in the account. Here's a sample letter that can be sent after the proposal or contract is signed and work is just beginning:

> Dear Joan:
>
> Thanks for the opportunity to work together. I'm looking forward to our partnership.
>
> I wonder if I might plant the idea for a small favor? Testimonials and endorsements are the coinage of my realm in this profession. Near the conclusion of our work together, when we're both delighted with the results, would you be willing to provide one or more of the following?

Action Items

> - A testimonial letter to be used with your peers in the future
>
> - A reference, used rarely, when a peer would like to talk directly
>
> - An endorsement for one of my book jackets
>
> - An interview for an article or newsletter
>
> Next time we're together, I'll check with you about these. In the meantime, thanks again for your support, and don't hesitate to call at any time.
>
> Sincerely,

You can add to, subtract from, or modify the list,[1] but you get the idea: Provide a "choice of yeses" very early and plant the seed. That way, you can learn early about resistance, opposing company policy, or whatever. Some people are happy to provide a letter and forget about it, but others don't like to commit anything to writing and prefer to be called. Go with the flow, but create some movement.

> Postgraduate Work #4: Buyers can support you in a number of ways, so encourage them to be creative with several options. Some will agree to all of them. The key is to establish the expectation early, then "call in your chip" when the time is right.

Testimonials are most effective in garnering additional business and/or establishing your credibility with new buyers when they adhere to the following.

The ten rules for effective testimonial letters:

They are:

- On company letterhead

- Addressed either to you or "To whom it may concern"

- Dated[2]

- Brief and to the point—two paragraphs are fine

- Include the buyer's name, title, and signature

- Cite your work and results (not merely your character and personality)

- Come from organizations recognizable by the prospect

- Clearly for paid engagements and not *pro bono* work

- All reproduced on common, high-quality paper, reproducing the original accurately (black and white reproduction is fine even for color logos and letterhead)

- Presented professionally as a book or coherent collection

Dissertation Assignment #1

Make a list of 20 people to call for referrals, with the objective of securing a minimum of 25 leads.

Send a letter to every client you've worked with during the past 18 months, requesting a testimonial letter.

Build into your proposal or contract procedure a follow-up letter similar to the one in this chapter preparing the buyer to provide a testimonial or reference of some kind.

The projected cost of doing this is almost zero. Your business acquisition should increase as a result, however, by at least 20 percent over the next year. Is that worth it?

Meet the challenge.

If you managed even one testimonial letter a month, you will be adding a dozen a year *and* will always have very current evidence to show a new prospect. There is simply no excuse for not requesting them.

---

[1]Note that I didn't include "provide referrals," because I think you should be gathering these regularly and immediately, not near the end of the project.

[2]Some people "white out" the dates so as to use "old" testimonials as if they were current. The trick is to have *a constant flow* of testimonials, so that the dates reveal quality work over a prolonged period.

Action Items

Some professionals like to provide a sample testimonial outline or even text to their clients. I find this to be much too stilted and manipulative. Instead, if you want to "prime the pump," after a client has agreed in concept, send them your current testimonial book and suggest that they can find examples from their peers that may give them some direction and ideas. That's highly effective in creating what you need without being overly aggressive.

> Postgraduate Work #5: You can create a table of contents for your testimonial book, which would indicate "Bank of America, page 5; Boston Consulting Group, page 6; . . ." Some prospects may simply want to check for similar industries, common geography, or organizations they respect.

Sponsorships

Sponsorships are often used by professional speakers, but are also effective in consulting and other professional disciplines. In many cases, there are organizations and prospects seriously interested in your help but legitimately without funds to pay for it.

In many cases, we automatically suggest a pro bono approach, particularly if we believe in the cause or are attracted to the project.[3] But I think there's a better way, which creates a "win/win/win" good deal.

The odds are that many of your past and present clients strongly support certain causes and initiatives. This could range from trade and professional associations to service clubs and charitable groups. Larger organizations, in fact, often have formal, budgeted funds set aside to provide grants, support, and other financial assistance. Some even provide "loaned" executives for up to a year to help manage the organization.

When you find a prospect that can use your help but can't afford your fees, consider these tactics:

---

[3]My criterion, by the way, is *never* to perform work pro bono for any profit-making organization.

Find out if they receive such support from other organizations

If they've received assistance from a corporate sponsor, then suggest that you be introduced with a strong endorsement for your work to receive such backing. This will enable you to:

- Treat the prospect as a typical client, and not one requiring "special favors" and lower priority.
- Meet some key people in the sponsoring organization that might also become a client.
- Effectively set up expectations for your intended work and the investment required.

Explore whether your current or past clients provide such subsidies

Ask your buyer if his or her company supports organizations in this way, and whether your expertise might be a part of the value provided. After all, you're a known quantity and there should be comfort that the investment in you is of the highest quality and very safe. This inquiry is important because:

- There may be such opportunity that you've never even explored.
- You might put the idea into your client's mind and create the business.
- It's an additional value proposition that you're providing.

> Post-Graduate Work #6: If you've never explored sponsorships at all, then you've probably either turned down business or taken it on for free. It can't hurt to at least ask the question and explore the three options provided here.

Investigate whether you can serve as intermediary to create sponsorship

If your prospect has no history of subsidy, and your own client base isn't offering it, then look into a possible match. For example, if your prospect is a nonprofit visiting nurse association that is undergoing terrible turnover

Action Items

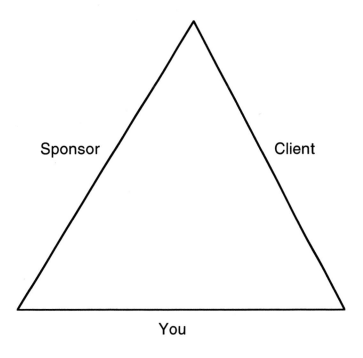

Figure 10-1: The "win/win/win" good deal

and a decline in quality of care, a pharmaceutical or therapeutic organization might find it attractive to provide your assistance for them. The benefits:

- Excellent public relations.

- Perhaps preferential consideration in buying decisions.

- Confidence that their products are being used correctly and well.

The key to a sponsorship is what I call the "good deal" triangle, which is shown in Figure 10-1.

If you can provide high value and positive outcomes to all parties, then you've created the "good deal." Some additional factors to consider:

- You can actually work with more than one sponsor on any given piece of business.

- You can work with one sponsor on multiple pieces of business.

- The sponsor must have no influence whatsoever on your work or professional relationship with the client. The sponsor must have a "hands off" attitude.

- The project should have the same kind of objectives, metrics, and specific value proposition that any project would have.

- You have a "buyer" in the client account, even though the actual funds originate externally.

- You should periodically apprise the sponsor of progress and seek to enlarge and enrich that relationship, as well.

Postgraduate Work #7: Some organizations continually sponsor professional help. Have you investigated the possibility of repeat engagements with such buyers? There is no reason why you can't be their permanent spokesperson, consultant, public relations option, and so on.

Action Items

A good source for sponsoring entities is within the trade association community. Inquire with the association whether any of its members assist the association itself, other nonprofits, or other members. You can also inquire within foundations established by large firms, with their public relations department, with their marketing people, and with local media sources.

Sales Stories

A bank that was insured not by the Federal Deposit Insurance Corporation, but by a state credit union, asked me to provide a management audit for the credit union and the other member banks. The bank requesting it of me had been a small client, and they were interested in the quality of the credit union management and the stability of the other banks.

The credit union readily accepted the "free" help, although less than half of the 12 member banks did. What I found was frightening in terms of poorly trained personnel, lax management practices, and sloppy follow-up.

The bank that hired me eventually left the credit union and secured membership with the FDIC. Was this a true sponsorship, when the bank had some very private interests in mind? I don't know how to categorize it, except to point out that these opportunities—outside of the paying customer's walls—are much more abundant than we suspect. The problem is that we don't pursue them.

Many consultants have told me of clients who paid them to work with their vendors, customers, and others in their value chain so as to ensure their own best interests—sort of a multifaceted "good deal."

In terms of sponsorships and related subsidies, learn to "think outside the walls." No organization can merely stand alone. Everyone needs suppliers, customers, intermediaries, sources, and so on. If it helps them to help their network of relationships, why shouldn't you be the one to provide the value?

One more idea in this general area: venture capitalist. Investors have a funny habit of wanting to safeguard their money. They are quite amenable to "due diligence" on a prospective acquisition, as well as monitoring existing assets. Someone is doing the financial audits, but who's doing the management audits? This is "sponsorship" of the most lucrative kind, because your fees are small compared to the insurance policy you provide on the proposed or current acquisition.

> Postgraduate Work #8: Ironically, the most important buyers are buyers who move from position to position. Track these people as you would a rainbow. At the end of your search is a real pot of gold.

Transient Buyers

I've never wished any buyer ill, but I do hope that some of them keep moving forever. Earlier in the book we discussed keeping in touch with everyone, past and present. If you do that diligently, you should "cleanse" your list in that most organizations will notify you when someone has departed or moved to another part of the company.

Your relationships are with people, not organizations. Hence, a buyer's nomadlike existence should be tracked with all the rigor of a dog tracking through the woods. Keep your nose to the ground and your ears perked up.

Buyers move for these reasons:

- Promotion
- Termination
- Downsizing
- Mergers/acquisitions
- Better offer elsewhere
- Retirement

Action Items

- Career change
- Transfer
- Spouse (new job, illness, family change, etc.)
- More desirable living conditions
- Temporary reassignment

Dissertation Assignment #2:

Create a list of all your buyers, organize a contact schedule, and implement it by next week. Also, go through your records and assemble all past buyers with whom you are no longer in contact, and begin tracking each one to add to your contact schedule.

You can accomplish this gradually over 30 days, or even have an assistant or part-time helper do it. The resultant list will serve to generate incremental business over the next year. There is no reason not to do this immediately.

Meet the challenge.

No matter what the reason—and some are positive, some negative, but it's not your job to be judgmental—here are some actions you can take or plan in order to maintain contact with every single buyer and with every single client opportunity.

Preventive Actions

1. Get the buyer's home phone in exchange for yours "in case of emergencies." Get the home address in order to send holiday cards. Normally, phone and mail are forwarded, sometimes for as long as a year.

2. Always establish a relationship with the buyer's direct reports. Someone among that group will usually be willing to tell you what happened and where the buyer went.

3. Establish a newsletter sent to the home or personal e-mail accounts of key contacts. E-mail addresses generally do not change.

4. Obviously, keep in touch minimally on a quarterly basis with past and current buyers, so that you don't wind up a year or more in arrears of any changes.

5. Make sure that the buyer has all of your contact information in various forms (press kit, Web site, business card, and so on) so that some will survive loss during a move and the buyer can readily find you.

Postgraduate Work #9: It's a good idea to use contact management software (or even a simple spreadsheet will do the trick) to keep track of individual buyers apart from the organizational and project contacts. Monitor how often you call, and set up reminders so that no more than, say, three months elapse between positive (not voice mail or e-mail) contacts.

Contingent Actions

1. Ask the direct reports and former secretary or assistant where the buyer is.

2. Ask people who were involved with you on your project's implementation.

3. Tell human resources that you have something that must be returned to the individual. (HR usually has forwarding information from severance agreements and so on, but refuses to provide it.)

4. Utilize all the home contact information: phone, street address, e-mail.

5. Use the Internet. It's often possible to turn up an individual with a good search engine, particularly if they have a Web site or belong to a variety of organizations. There are also Web sites that claim anyone can be tracked (for a fee).

Why is it so important to keep tabs on buyers? Because they tend to buy again. I've worked with buyers who have brought me into no less than six organizations during their career, and some who even have recommended me to former contacts, *after they had retired themselves.* That's why I listed such a diversity of reasons for departure above. It doesn't really matter why they leave or where they go: No one can help you as much as someone who has already (happily) purchased your services.

The "chase" is worthwhile, because the cost of acquisition will still be less than that of trying to penetrate a completely new account. And don't kid yourself—many buyers don't have your contact information memorized, are preoccupied during a move, and are thinking "I wonder how I could get what's-his-name involved with this new project?" The trouble is, that thought will vanish unless we find the thinker.

Action Items

Keep tabs on everyone who has ever purchased anything from you. It will be a discipline and pursuit that will pay off in incremental business. Woody Allen said that "80 percent of success is in just showing up." Find a way to show up.

> Postgraduate Work #10: Go through the "notes" pages in this book and collect your reminders and ideas. Choose three things to work on immediately. Nothing happens until you take accountability for your own improvement. Start now.

NOTE TO READERS: There is a CD-ROM affixed to the inside cover of this book that contains a sales conversation between me and a buyer. We tackle objections, rebuttals, fee demands, value propositions, objectives, options, and a great deal more. I've created this in response to continuing demand for such a sample of my "conversational selling" approach. The CD is not a reiteration of the book's material, but rather provides examples via role-plays and small "dramas" for how you implement the ideas in a practical manner. I hope you enjoy it.

Final Sales Story

I began my own practice in 1985 and, in my first full year, made $125,000 (in 1986 dollars). I never looked back, and was making seven figures at the time I published my best-seller, *Million Dollar Consulting,* in 1992.

I don't like to "sell." I'm an introvert. I don't like to "prove myself" to others. So, I created the strategies and tactics you've read in these pages to overcome my vulnerabilities and instead play to my strengths—use of the language, ability to frame issues, organization, and time efficiency.

My advice is for you to adopt those devices that maximize your strengths. I don't claim that my way is the best way or that my approaches must be adopted in their entirety. But there have to be ideas in this book that will work for you, and that will help you earn much more money in much less time.

All I can tell you is that I've done it, continue to do it, and look forward to doing it even better tomorrow.

Self-assessment

How well are you:

- Gaining referrals from every single client?
- Generating testimonials?
- Gaining references?
- Acquiring sponsorships?
- Tracking and selling to transient buyers?

Summary of the Postgraduate Work

Postgraduate Work #1: Ask every current client for referral business at least once a quarter. Period. If you're not doing that, then you're working very hard to go around the block in order to get next door.

Postgraduate Work #2: Refer potential business to your clients where possible, and make that act known (whether it results in business or not). Then you will have "greased the reciprocal skids."

Postgraduate Work #3: If you find that a pleasant and cordial meeting will not result in business for quite sound reasons, but the relationship is good, try this: "I'm sorry we won't be able to work together, but I'm confident we understand each other's situation. Before I leave, could you recommend to me three or four people who may be able to benefit from my services, now knowing what you know about me?" There is nothing to lose, and you'll usually walk out of an "unsuccessful" sales call with three new leads!

Action Items

Postgraduate Work #4: Buyers can support you in a number of ways, so encourage them to be creative with several options. Some will agree to all of them. The key is to establish the expectation early, then "call in your chip" when the time is right.

Postgraduate Work #5: You can create a table of contents for your testimonial book, which would indicate "Bank of America, page 5; Boston Consulting Group, page 6; . . ." Some prospects may simply want to check for similar industries, common geography, or organizations they respect.

Postgraduate Work #6: If you've never explored sponsorships at all, then you've probably either turned down business or taken it on for free. It can't hurt to at least ask the question and explore the three options provided here.

Postgraduate Work #8: Ironically, the most important buyers are buyers who move from position to position. Track these people as you would a rainbow. At the end of your search is a real pot of gold.

Postgraduate Work #9: It's a good idea to use contact management software (or even a simple spreadsheet will do the trick) to keep track of individual buyers apart from the organizational and project contacts. Monitor how often you call, and set up reminders so that no more than, say, three months elapse between positive (not voice mail or e-mail) contacts.

Postgraduate Work #10: Go through the "notes" pages in this book and collect your reminders and ideas. Choose three things to work on immediately. Nothing happens until you take the accountability for your own improvement. Start now.

Action Items

Summary of Chapter Self-assessments and Sales Skills Courses

Chapter 1
Self-assessment

To what extent are you:

- Engaged in areas in which there is market need, for which you have competencies, and about which you have great passion?

- Self-assured and confident, having made the first sale to yourself, so that low self-esteem is not an extra sales obstacle?

- Thinking of the fourth sale first, building relationships and enduring business rather than "closes," brief events, and one-time sales?

- Thinking from the outside in, so that you can identify the buyer's self-interest and cater to that emotional trigger?

- Establishing needs and not just responding to wants, thereby increasing the perception of your unique value added?

Summary of Sales Skills 100

Sales Skills 101: The more people perceive a need, the easier to sell your alternative to meet that need. The less people perceive a need, the more you must help them feel that need before you can sell your alternative. Need precedes purchase.

Sales Skills 102: Logic makes people think, emotion makes them act. No matter what the product or service, if you can touch the "emotional trigger" of the buyer, the sales will be both accelerated and enhanced. You can easily be too intellectual to make a sale.

Sales Skills 103: The greatest failure of salespeople is to be unconvinced (and, therefore, unconvincing). If you don't believe it, don't do it. The point isn't to "make a sale." The point is to establish a relationship that leads to many sales. Personal belief precedes buyer acceptance.

Sales Skills 104: Never enter a prospect's presence unless you are absolutely convinced that you have what he or she needs, and that you can significantly improve the prospect's well-being. If you don't believe it, then change your market, change your product, or change your attitude.

Sales Skills 105: Always understand where you are in your own sales model. That way, you know which small "yes" should be the next target. In this manner, you control the buying dynamic, not the buyer. In every interaction with a true buyer, a sale is made. The critical consideration is that you be the one making it.

Sales Skills 106: If you're discussing price, you've lost control of the discussion. Early discussions should be only about *value*. People may buy based on lowest price, but they engage in long-term relationships over value. Salespeople should have value propositions, not sales propositions or, worse, fee propositions.

Sales Skills 107: Always determine "what's in it for her." You know what's in it for you. The idea is to convert your self-interest into the client self-interest, *so that there is a reciprocity of interests*. A "sale" of a training program is strictly in your self-interest. Improved retention rates are in both your self-interests.

Sales Skills 108: When the client says, "I've been rattling on for quite some time," or "We're almost out of time and you really haven't had a chance to say anything," you've been highly successful. You'll never find a prospect sneak a peek at his watch or have her eyes glaze over while the prospect is speaking . . .

Sales Skills 109: Have someone "shop" your own practice and give you feedback. How easy is it to leave a message, obtain information, use your Web site? The answers will inevitably provide direction in "thinking from the outside in."

Sales Skills 110: If you can't, at any given time, summarize the other person's viewpoint and observations up to that juncture, you just haven't been listening carefully. Summarize mentally as you listen and you'll find that you're considered a great thinker.

Chapter 2
Self-assessment

To what extent are you:

- Identifying your buyers' comfort zones?
- Providing the types of assurances and reactions each style finds most attractive?
- Anticipating and preventing the four major areas of resistance?
- Engaging the buyer in conversation to build trust, need, and urgency?
- Eliminating the validity of "no money" based on other needs?

Summary of Sales Skills 200

Sales Skills 201: There is nothing new under the sales sun, and that includes buyers' objections to whatever it is you're selling. Unfortunately, most sales professionals concentrate on emphasizing features and benefits rather than responding to specific buyer objections. The former are for you; the latter are for the person who can sign your check.

Sales Skills 202: People will tend to object to change in areas consistent with their social behaviors. That is, you are more likely to get a response of "no money" from an analytic, detailed person than you are from someone who thrives on gaining results, no matter what. Therefore, understanding your buyer's style is a prerequisite to preventing objections.

Sales Skills 203: One's style is always valid. Don't make value judgments, and don't mistake the descriptors for "labels." The idea is not to "explain away" behavior, but to try to understand it so that you can anticipate problems and exploit strengths.

Sales Skills 204: The four basic social styles will tend to display themselves in a variety of obvious and subtle ways, from choices of language to physical behavior and surroundings. Once you notice a pattern, the key is to adapt to the buyer's style, not to remain resolutely in your own. All of us are capable of such movement around the quadrants, but the buyer has no incentive to do so. You do.

Sales Skills 205: If you know what's likely to happen, there is no excuse for not being prepared. You take an umbrella when you're told to expect rain, and you take along your appropriate arguments and advantages when you know to expect "We don't have the money (or the time, or the need, or the trust)." If you don't, you get soaked—and you deserve it.

Sales Skills 206: In the great preponderance of cases, you have to demonstrate need. Not everyone will be as anxious or able to see it as you. The better your relationship, no matter how long it takes to develop, the better the chance that the buyer will be willing to give you the benefit of the doubt.

Sales Skills 207: Once gained and lost, trust is virtually impossible to reacquire. It's shattered when either party abrogates its terms, because each party has invested an emotional component. "You let me down" is one of the most serious accusations that we encounter in business, because it clearly implies that you'll let me down again in the future if you have the chance.

Sales Skills 208: There is really no such thing as "no time." There is, however, such a thing as "low priority."

Sales Skills 209: There is no such thing as "no money." There is always money. The only question is to whom the check is written. In any major organization, in particular, if you accept "no money" or "no budget," you might as well go into another line of work. Sales is not for you.

Sales Skills 210: If you prepare for the four fundamental resistance areas, you should be able to close most sales with most buyers. And the quality and amounts of those sales will be larger than average.

Chapter 3
Self-assessment

To what extent are you:

- Defining your value as a business outcome for the buyer?

- Translating inputs (tasks) into outputs (results)?

- Providing tangible measures of progress?

- Identifying and reaching the true buyer?

- Effectively eliminating gatekeepers?

Summary of Sales Skills 300

Sales Skills 301: Your value is important only in terms of a buyer's perceived outcomes. The "things that you do" at best have a temporary appeal. It's the "things that you produce" that linger after your departure, that have permanence in terms of value for the buyer.

Sales Skills 302: The only person qualified and possessing the requisite knowledge to translate your unique background into the client's desired future is you. If you don't take pains to do this, *no one else is capable of or interested in doing it.* Why keep the secret?

Sales Skills 303: Progress points and measures of improvement not only provide comfort for the buyer, but also provide leverage points for the seller to generate more business. This is because the progress points serve as interim demonstrations of success, and you can be a hero prior to the actual completion of the project.

Sales Skills 304: "If you can't measure it, you can't manage it," might be extreme, but "If you can't measure it, you can't convince the buyer you had anything to do with it," is a somewhat more accurate and sobering thought.

Sales Skills 305: The greatest danger in ignoring measures of improvement is that the project is screamingly successful, and the buyer says, "You know, you're a pleasure to work with, but I'm not so sure we wouldn't have accomplished this on our own in any case." At that point, you have effectively been rendered mute and, not incidentally, devoid of repeat business.

Sales Skills 306: Blockers are paid to block you. Economic buyers are paid to get results. The first group is successful when they deny you the opportunity to interact with a true buyer. If you voluntarily spend time with them, you are plotting your own demise.

Sales Skills 307: Don't try to find the economic buyer through the criteria of who is evaluating the external resources. That job is often "tasked" to gatekeepers. Instead, find out who is responsible for funding, timing, and results. That person will be your true buyer.

Sales Skills 308: Your job is about closing business, not making people like you or being overly concerned with everyone's feelings. If you are consumed with everyone liking you, then stand on the street corner and give away money. But if you're concerned about acquiring customers and clients, then don't be afraid to charge past a gatekeeper. You can always break down, scale, burrow under, or otherwise circumvent any gate.

Sales Skills 309: It is sometimes uncomfortable and disquieting to upset a gatekeeper. Of course, that pain is nothing compared to not getting the business or, worse, wasting months of your time before not getting the business. If gatekeepers stop you, you are using the wrong tactics, under the wrong impression, or in the wrong business.

Sales Skills 310: Gatekeepers are empowered and enabled by docility. It is, literally, either them or you. It is more than a little ironic to expect to make a sale to an economic buyer but be waylaid by a gatekeeper. Try to convince them quickly of the need to meet the buyer but, failing that, blast through. They are not called "impenetrable fortress keepers."

Chapter 4
Self-assessment

To what extent are you:

- Seeking the core resistance and isolating that factor for resolution?
- Employing turnaround tactics?
- Adding information to bring a "no" back to neutral?
- Avoiding being placed on the defensive and resorting to price or fee?
- Maintaining strong buyer relationships even after a "no"?

Summary of Sales Skills 400

Sales Skills 401: Buyer volume, objection, and vocal resistance are *positives*. If the buyer didn't care at all, he or she wouldn't bother to protest so vehemently. Temporary issues may separate you, but common passion is sufficient to unite positions if you can find the right opportunity and use the right techniques to make this happen during the relationship-building process.

Sales Skills 402: Many buyers don't know what their real fear is. They require help to identify and articulate it. In many cases, the fear isn't even real, or can be dealt with easily with a few guarantees. But you won't know this unless you take the time to isolate the true resistance factor.

Sales Skills 403: The "ambiguous zone" can appear anywhere. Never attempt to combat an amorphous mass. Keep driving toward the real barrier. Once you do that, you can convert the buyer's passionate resistance to passionate support.

Sales Skills 404: Never feel compelled to respond to a question just because it's authoritative (the hallmark of drivers) or loud. And never step into silences, however awkward they are. You'll always—ALWAYS—say something you'll regret, and if it's at all about fees, you'll usually rue the day.

Sales Skills 405: Practice turnaround tactics in "safe" situations to become proficient. If someone says, "What do you think you're doing?" reply, "I don't know, what do you think I'm doing?" The defensiveness is immediately removed. Warning: Do not try this with your spouse.

Sales Skills 406: Don't be depressed by a "no." Simply regard it as any other objection and use the techniques designed to change it. You'll need an emotional trigger to bring the buyer at least back to neutral. That's easier—and safer—than going from "drive" to "reverse" without an intermediate stop.

Sales Skills 407: Never take it personally. It's almost always not personal. If you disregard your own ego and focus on the buyer's ego, you have a good chance of eventually reversing any objection. If you focus on your own ego and ignore the buyer's ego, you have a good chance of immediately hitting the pavement.

Sales Skills 408: You may lose a sale (the battle) but you never have to lose a buyer's relationship (the war). The ancient Greeks believed in heroic death, while the Romans believed in living to fight another day. The Romans, of course, thoroughly defeated the Greeks. Do you get my drift?

Sales Skills 409: The buyers are the roads leading to sales destinations. You might not always reach the destination quickly or on a single road. But if you're smart, you'll invest in keeping the roads well maintained and easily accessible.

Sales Skills 410: Your relationship is with the buyer, not the organization. Pursue and follow the buyer. Buyers can take you with them to new conditions and new environments. Organizations usually can't.

Chapter 5
Self-assessment

How well are you:

- Providing a viable set of options (at every point in the sale)?
- Finding comparisons that place your project into a very reasonable perspective?
- Avoiding the purchasing department at all costs?
- Playing to emotions to force both early action and deep commitment?
- Actively managing the majority of the sales dynamic and preparing to do so prior to your discussions?

Summary of Sales Skills 500

Sales Skills 501: Offering options is a method of involving the buyer in the diagnostic of how to approach the project. Moreover, options induce a buyer to advance up the value chain. You are negligent if you are not including options in every proposal. *Every proposal.*

Sales Skills 502: All buyers love to reduce fees, but no buyer wants to reduce value. By escalating your value proposition you'll create irresistible upward pressure on fees. You control this entire dynamic.

Sales Skills 503: Of course there's "no money." No one awakes in the morning and says, "Let me find a way to budget money for Alan Weiss in case we have need of his services." Moreover, if a client can "find" $50,000, she can find $150,000. Do not go gentle into that good night . . .

Sales Skills 504: Some of the most useful comparisons can involve the buyer's own prior expectations. We often find ourselves in worlds of diminished expectations and necessary evils. Sometimes we can help the buyer to rediscover the loftier, more important priorities.

Sales Skills 505: Purchasing agents are paid to conserve funds, remain within budget, and generally reduce expenditures. Why on earth would you want to deal with someone with that responsibility? Line managers and executives are paid to generate results. Don't waste time on the input and cost side when you could be on the output and value side. That's where the big money is.

Sales Skills 506: Bureaucratic rules can work both ways. By offering modest inducements, you can actually trigger a Pavlovian purchasing department response to pay you quickly, or make electronic deposits, or pay in advance for expenses. After a while, you stop feeling guilty.

Sales Skills 507: The way to influence behavior in your favor is to appeal to the other person's rational self-interest. Demonstrate to the buyer that the purchasing department will be a detriment to timing, ROI, expediency, and so on. Place the onus on the buyer to resolve that issue. The probability is strong that the buyer has experienced delays and problems in that area before. Build on that history.

Sales Skills 508: When all else fails, follow instructions: Find the emotional triggers that will compel the buyer to act. Don't waste time on logic and thinking. There is absolutely no embarrassment in being an "impulse purchase" if the buyer has the impulse—and means—to spend $150,000 on something that means a lot to him.

Sales Skills 509: Emotional needs will be expressed as a result of trust. Trust is established during the course of relationship-building. Relationships are based on mutual disclosure. Hence, revealing your own emotional triggers will support this process and accelerate it.

Sales Skills 510: The seller controls the preponderance of the buying dynamic. How ironic it is that the buyer exerts more influence while controlling the minority of the interaction. Make the best use of your weapons, and your best weapons are offensive, not defensive.

Chapter 6
Self-assessment

How well are you:

- Sensitive to further improvements as you begin a project?
- Reaching out laterally to meet new buyers?
- Creating a "good deal" for your buyer and yourself?
- Confident that you can help the buyer meet emotional needs?
- Offering free advice that becomes trust for major projects?

Summary of Sales Skills 600

Sales Skills 601: To garner repeat business, you must provide quality work and solid service. But you also have to *ask for it*. Many firms do the first two, and then forget the third.

Sales Skills 602: Don't view your role as one of project implementer. See yourself as a partner of the buyer, as interested in and informed about his business as he is. Actively look for and suggest alternatives to improve the client condition and the buyer's situation. Ask yourself, "What would I do if I were running this place?"

Sales Skills 603: Sales is about providing value in return for equitable compensation. If you believe that, then you're negligent in not offering services and products to someone who will be legitimately improved by applying them, and requesting fair recompense for that transfer. If you don't believe that your services can help the buyer, then you have no business selling them.

Sales Skills 604: View your customer as the center of a universe of lateral buying opportunities, then assess which presents you with the best opportunities. Never view any buyer or any client as a singular and narrow experience.

Sales Skills 605: If you're not plotting the totality of the sales potential for ongoing business acquisition right from the outset, then you're not completing your sales accountability. After all the work and expense of business acquisition, why ignore the true business potential?

Sales Skills 606: If you view additional opportunities as things you're "selling" to a buyer, you're creating an adversarial relationship. If you view them, instead, as additional value for the buyer (improvements in his or her condition), then you're creating a partnering relationship. The choice, and the business, is yours.

Sales Skills 607: When you don't raise issues, either assuming that the buyer is already aware or fearful of the perception you'll create, you're doing neither the buyer nor yourself a favor. Professional salespeople don't fear sales opportunities. You don't make rain by standing under an umbrella.

Sales Skills 608: Your alternatives are to put your feet on the street, metaphorically, and beat down new doors, or to put your feet up on the client's ottoman and suggest some additional ways for your partner to succeed. Is there really a debate about which is easier, more productive, and more rewarding? You'll get plenty of chances to beat down doors. Why forfeit the chance to help your current partner succeed, and for both of you to profit? We're not talking ethics, we're talking business sense.

Sales Skills 609: Free advice is not of little value. The client is paying for it, since you've already been engaged. The key is to ensure that the advice can be immediately utilized and the wisdom appreciated.

Sales Skills 610: If you can't generate more business while you're actively partnering with a trusting buyer, then you just aren't trying. Most lost opportunity is due to consultant fear or reluctance, not buyer intransigence. And that is the traditional "good news/bad news."

Chapter 7
Self-assessment

How well are you:

- Solidifying your position and relationship with the buyer on an ongoing basis?

- Being perceived as a "part of the client's team"?

- Developing short-term measures and successes?

- Protecting yourself against perceived diminished returns in the future?

- Using a networking map to exploit all potential client business?

Summary of Sales Skills 700

Sales Skills 701: Make no mistake about it: You face a far greater threat from internal client dynamics and opposition than you ever do from external consulting competition. Yet we are much more alert to and prepared for the latter than the former.

Sale Skills 702: After the hard work of reaching a buyer and closing business, to abandon that relationship is like climbing Mount Everest and deciding not to look at the view before heading down again. Abandon the peak at your own peril, because most people don't make the climb a second time.

Sales Skills 703: Team members support each other, establish rapport, suffer common defeats, and rejoice in common victories. A team stands together. If you are a part of such a team, let the momentum sweep you past the rapids and into the deep, blue water.

Sales Skills 704: Not only will you become part of the team by attending ongoing meetings, but you will also quickly learn the often hidden dynamics of power, influence, and persuasion that the key players exert with one another. You may just find that you've missed the true power brokers by looking at title instead of influence.

Sales Skills 705: If you're going to be part of a team, contribute. Don't sit back and watch. The more you actively help the group, the more you'll learn, the more you'll be accepted, and the more you'll be engaged long-term.

Sales Skills 706: Too few consultants go to the buyer regularly and ask, as New York City's Mayor Koch used to ask pedestrians on their way to work, "How am I doing?" They seem to allow the fear of "bad" feedback to destroy their chances of gaining positive and important feedback to validate their contribution.

Sales Skills 707: There will occasionally be resistors and threatened people who gather evidence on problems and contradictions about any project. We tend to spend too much time dueling with them. By compiling your own documentation of successes and small victories, you'll have ample validation for your buyer that things are proceeding ahead of plan, and that the inevitable resistance to change has inevitably surfaced.

Sales Skills 708: If you don't blow your own horn, there is no music. Or, as baseball pitcher and Hall of Fame member Dizzy Dean once said, "If you can do it, it ain't braggin'."

Sales Skills 709: View your relationships in an account as "internal networking." Just as you network to attract business as a part of normal marketing efforts, do the same thing internally, within existing clients. The process is exactly the same, except you have the advantage of being known and trusted inside the client.

Sales Skills 710: It is a reasonable expectation that any client can engage you for a multiplicity of projects over several years. These are not events, but rather relationships. The greatest detriment to obtaining frequent and ongoing business is the consultant. The client is actually quite willing.

Chapter 8
Self-assessment

How well are you:

- Maintaining contact with all past buyers and significant others?

- Establishing contact with new buyers in existing and recent clients?

- "Mining" past clients for the possibility of revival?

- Bringing new value, new approaches, and new talents to the attention of past buyers?

- Protecting yourself in current engagements against poor experiences?

Summary of Sales Skills 800

Sales Skills 801: You can make all buyers, past and present, *contemporary relationships* by never surrendering the initiative to remain in contact. That is the key preventive action to avoid clients from disappearing and your off-balance-sheet asset from becoming worthless.

Sales Skills 802: The line between follow-up and "hunting" is not a thin one. If you're constantly out for yourself only and trying to secure additional business, the client will need the ghostbusters. But if you're regularly supplying value and help for the buyer's business, you're engaged in very professional follow-up and the chances are strong that no one will be slimed.

Sales Skills 803: While the buyer constitutes your personal relationship, the organization is part of your business relationship, and you can use that to establish contact with new buyers. However, you have to start from scratch with your personal relationship-building. In fact, you might be starting from less than scratch.

Sales Skills 804: When the old buyer disappears, for whatever reason, start to train the heavy artillery on the new buyer. Use every bit of your knowledge and experience with the organization to create more value for him or her. If you don't blow your own horn, there is no music.

Sales Skills 805: Buyers can readily resist "old" consultants associated with past regimes. But they can't wait to get their hands on "new" value, unexpected help, which might get them off to a running start in their new position. Don't position yourself, position the value to the buyer. It's not about your past, it's about the buyer's future.

Sales Skills 806: There are either clients or nonclients. Of the former, some are active and some are inactive. There is no limbo. Most consultants make virtually no attempt to turn inactive clients into active clients, which is always easier than turning nonclients into clients.

Sales Skills 807: With past clients, drop names and events. Tie yourself to successful innovations and initiatives. Use names of people who have been promoted or who left under very favorable circumstances. But don't tie yourself to regimes fallen out of favor or projects that sputtered and crashed. Do your homework before showing up in class.

Sales Skills 808: It's not that you've failed, it's how you intend to recover. It's not that you've been unfairly blamed or treated, it's how you handle it. It's not what happens to you, it's what you do about it.

Sales Skills 809: Some buyers will attempt to use you as the "club" that they, themselves, are unwilling to bear on their staff or peers. Never take on a project that is a "vendetta" or in which you are the pry bar. We want to create light, but not be the flash point.

Sales Skills 810: I've never been in any major project in which conditions didn't change and the unexpected didn't crop up. Agility is far more important than systemization, and nimble can be better than rigid on almost any occasion. Constantly deploy and check your radar for new blips on the screen. They may not be friendly and may not be enemy: They may just be storm clouds so severe that you need to find the eye of the storm.

Chapter 9
Self-assessment

How well are you:

- Asking for retainer arrangements?
- Establishing mutually beneficial guidelines for retainer relationships?
- Increasing your retainer business as a percentage of revenues?
- Balancing project and retainer work?
- Minimizing your travel and the onerous parts of your delivery?

Summary of Sales Skills 900

Sales Skills 901: The retainer arrangement is actually sometimes the solution to a buyer's problem about how to use you more but minimize the resistance and/or bureaucracy in his own organization. Retainers must always be "win/win."

Sales Skills 902: It's always possible to suggest a conversion to a retainer arrangement. The worst the client can say is "no." The key is to present the conversion as particularly timely, economical, and effective. You are probably the only person in a position to possess all the facts to make this case.

Sales Skills 903: Retainer work is subject to "midcourse" alteration more than is project work. Expect it, and prepare your buyer for it. It is inadvertently easy for a client to abuse a retainer relationship, *as it is for a consultant to pay insufficient attention to it.* By open communications and through trust, you can avoid both pitfalls.

Sales Skills 904: Projects have defined goals and metrics, and end when those measures indicate the goals are accomplished. Retainers have defined time frames and limited access. They end when the calendar indicates they've expired.

Sales Skills 905: The key to a project is to be specifically effective in a narrow scope. The key to a retainer is to be generally effective in a wide scope. Neither is mutually exclusive, but these are two separate competencies.

Sales Skills 906: Establish the rules of the road early, or you'll soon be having disagreements over the best route to the destination. You might naturally choose the fastest alternative, while the buyer might prefer the scenic tour. You have to agree on the criteria.

Sales Skills 907: The line between retainer work and project work is clear and should be drawn in the sand. Once you're asked to proceed beyond advice and actually oversee implementation (e.g., project planning, monitoring, midcourse correction, and so on), you've left the retainer farm and headed for the big city. The big city is much more expensive.

Sales Skills 908: There is nothing immoral or unethical or illegal about minimizing physical time present in retainer work. The only question is: Am I living up to my obligations and the expectations of the buyer? Technology and retainer work were made for each other.

Sales Skills 909: The successful professional should have a strategy to create more and more retainer assignments, and to orient marketing initiatives, collateral materials, and, most important, buyer conversations in that direction.

Sales Skills 910: You will seldom receive retainers if you don't ask for them. You will seldom be able to ask for one without a strong, pre-existing relationship. That is still another reason why effective selling is a relationship business.

Chapter 10
Self-assessment

How well are you:

- Gaining referrals from every single client?

- Generating testimonials?

- Gaining references?

- Acquiring sponsorships?

- Tracking and selling to transient buyers?

Summary of the Postgraduate Work

Postgraduate Work #1: Ask every current client for referral business at least once a quarter. Period. If you're not doing that, then you're working very hard to go around the block in order to get next door.

Postgraduate Work #2: Refer potential business to your clients where possible, and make that act known (whether it results in business or not). Then you will have "greased the reciprocal skids."

Postgraduate Work #3: If you find that a pleasant and cordial meeting will not result in business for quite sound reasons, but the relationship is good, try this: "I'm sorry we won't be able to work together, but I'm confident we understand each other's situation. Before I leave, could you recommend to me three or four people who may be able to benefit from my services, now knowing what you know about me?" There is nothing to lose, and you'll usually walk out of an "unsuccessful" sales call with three new leads!

Postgraduate Work #4: Buyers can support you in a number of ways, so encourage them to be creative with several options. Some will agree to all of them. The key is to establish the expectation early, then "call in your chip" when the time is right.

Postgraduate Work #5: You can create a table of contents for your testimonial book, which would indicate "Bank of America, page 5; Boston Consulting Group, page 6; . . ." Some prospects may simply want to check for similar industries, common geography, or organizations they respect.

Postgraduate Work #6: If you've never explored sponsorships at all, then you've probably either turned down business or taken it on for free. It can't hurt to at least ask the question and explore the three options provided here.

Postgraduate Work #7: Some organizations continually sponsor professional help. Have you investigated the possibility of repeat engagements with such buyers? There is no reason why you can't be their permanent spokesperson, consultant, public relations option, and so on.

Postgraduate Work #8: Ironically, the most important buyers are buyers who move from position to position. Track these people as you would a rainbow. At the end of your search is a real pot of gold.

Postgraduate Work #9: It's a good idea to use contact management software (or even a simple spreadsheet will do the trick) to keep track of individual buyers apart from the organizational and project contacts. Monitor how often you call, and set up reminders so that no more than, say, three months elapse between positive (not voice mail or e-mail) contacts.

Postgraduate Work #10: Go through the "notes" pages in this book and collect your reminders and ideas. Choose three things to work on immediately. Nothing happens until you take accountability for your own improvement. Start now.